CW01627137

Llandudno and the Mostyn Influence

AUXILIUM MEUM A DOMINO

• • •

HEB DDUW, HEB DDIM, DUW A DIGON

• • •

WITHOUT GOD, WITHOUT ANYTHING,
GOD IS ENOUGH

Llandudno from the Great Orme

An Historical Account
of
Llandudno and the Mostyn Influence

by
F. Ron Williams B.Sc., A.F.I.M.A.

Mostyn Estate
and
Llandudno and District Historical Society
1996

Llandudno from the Little Orme

Text © F. Ron Williams 1996

Copyright © by T.Davies & Son (NW) Ltd. t/a Catalist 1996.
All right reserved.
No part of this publication may be reproduced or
transmitted, in any form or by any means, without permission.

ISBN 1-898202-06-0

Cover design:
Astrid Williams and Bernard Norrie

Cover Picture:
Mostyn Street in the early 1860's

First published in 1996 by:
Catalist, Albert House, Albert Drive, Deganwy, Conwy LL31 9RL
Telephone: 01492-584682

Printed by:
Rhos Press, 1 Claughton Road, Colwyn Bay, Conwy LL29 7EF
Telephone: 01492-535900

Contents

Chapter	Page
Contents	v
Preface	vi
Introduction by Roy Orr	vii
Introduction by Peter Caldwell	viii
The Early Mostyns	1
The Mostyn Knights and Baronets	3
The Lloyd Succession	8
Uneasy Years	10
Llandudno before Inclosure	18
Enclosure and Llandudno	26
Public Auction and Planned Development	33
The Parliamentary Acts for Llandudno of 1853 and 1854	39
The Llandudno Commissioners: Early Years	43
The Essential Services for Llandudno	47
Housing and Streets	55
Regulations and 'Nuisances': Policing and Controls	63
The Esplanade in Early Days	68
Chapels, Churches and Schools	73
Other Important Buildings	80
Gloddaeth and Bodysgallen	85
Llandudno in 1861: An Assessment	89
Appendices & Genealogical Tables	
The Early Mostyns	94
The Mostyn Knights and Baronets	95
The Lloyd Succession	96
The Lloyds	97
The Mostyn Barons	98
The Early Churches	99
List of Illustrations	100
Subject Index	101

Author's Preface

In presenting this first part of the history of Llandudno and the Mostyn Influence I am conscious of the fact that some future historian may seek to modify some of the personal views and conclusions expressed, for I have, of necessity, been selective in my consideration of the very large number of documents which are available relating to the Mostyn family. However, that is for the future, and I am content to have made a start to the subject.

There are five main sources which have been consulted. Two of these are where much material relating to the Mostyns has been deposited, namely, the Clwyd Archives at Hawarden and the U.C.N.W. Archives at Bangor. This Mostyn archival material relates to estates in many parts of both Wales and England, as well as comprising much that is concerned with more general family matters. It is thus very relevant to acknowledge the Archivists' work in cataloguing and titling the deposited material. It was only by reference to these catalogues that I was able to select items thought to be relevant to Llandudno and thus keep the study of these fascinating documents down to a manageable number, measured in hundreds, rather than in many thousands.

A third source of information has been the Gwynedd County Record Office at Caernarfon, where there is much deposited relating to Llandudno, including the Improvement Commissioners' Minute Books. My thanks are extended to the staff of this establishment and also to those of the local library in Llandudno, my fourth source of information, where there is interesting material in the reference section.

The fifth major source is, of course, the office of the Mostyn estate, where I was given free access to browse through the files in the record room. Many visits were made over a lengthy period and much of the material obtained from here will, I believe, prove to be of greatest value for the preparation of the second part of this narrative.

So much for the sources, but why, it may be asked, was the task undertaken in the first place? I can only answer this by writing that as a native of Llandudno and a visitor to the town every year throughout my working life, it seemed a suitable place for retirement – a view that was agreed to by my wife, after due consideration of the various options available. Membership of the Llandudno and District Historical Society followed and when, as its Secretary, I made contact with the Estate Office on some matter, this, in turn, led to the arrangement with the then agent, Mr.Roy Orr.

In conclusion, I would like to acknowledge the help and encouragement received from the three Mostyn Agents that it has been my pleasure to meet, these being George Hiller, Roy Orr and the present agent Peter Caldwell. Thanks are also due to the numerous friends who share my interest in matters historical, and in particular to Tom Parry, Stanley Wicklen, Roland Pickering, David Atkinson and Elan and Stuart Rivers. Lastly I must record my thanks to my wife, Astrid, for her patience and forebearance on the many occasions when I have seemed more concerned with the past than with the present.

Introduction by Roy Orr

When I took over from George Hiller, who had been Chief Agent for the 28 years prior to 1987, I was surprised that the Mostyn Estate had no written history of its role in the development of Llandudno.

George Hiller has a vast fund of knowledge which he had acquired from many sources but I am sure he would be the first to agree that much of it was anecdotal.

With his retirement in 1987 there was a risk that a lot of the information would be lost and I felt that during my term of office, albeit a much shorter period of just over 7 years, A history should be prepared.

I turned to Ron Williams and the Llandudno and District Historical Society to ask them to prepare such a document with the instruction that the history should be published "warts and all". I felt that a bland and edited document would not do justice to what was a major achievement by our Victorian forbears and which, like most worthy achievements, was not arrived at without problems.

The document is to be published in two parts. The first covers the period up to 1861, this date being something of a watershed in the Estate's history. The second part will be from 1861 to 1940. It was a matter of some debate as to the date that the history should terminate but 1940 seemed to be logical because most of the basic structure of the town was well established by that time and really the Estate did not play much of an active role during the war years.

I am grateful to Ron Williams and the Society for the amount of time and trouble that has been given to the project and I hope it will serve as a fair report of a major private initiative in land development and subsequent land stewardship over a period of 150 years.

R.R.Orr
Chief Agent 1987-1995

As the current Chief Agent of the Estate I am acutely aware of the great sense of history that is attached to the Estate. I never cease to be amazed at the foresight and the boldness of the Mostyn Family and it is a privilege to be the custodian of such a successful heritage.

I look forward to taking this forward into the new millenium for the benefit of the town of Llandudno.

P.J.R.Caldwell

Church Walks

Whilst it is not the intention of the author to attempt a comprehensive history of the Mostyn family it is of course necessary for the purposes of this book to make reference to them, and to relevant genealogical tables, in order to relate the family to their various estates, and particularly those in the Llandudno area.

The Mostyn lineage can with certainty be followed back well into the Middle Ages, and the line of succession is shown in the appendices to this book. The standard reference source of such information is of course Burke[1] but in this case it can be greatly supplemented by a history of the Mostyn Family written in 1925 and co-authored by the third Baron Mostyn[2]. Only 154 copies of this book were printed, its preface stating its purpose as being "the preservation in a concise form for the information of descendants an account of the family of Mostyn of Mostyn". There is much in this book that deserves a wider readership, including information relating to the Llandudno area.

It was in the fifteenth century that Ieuan Fychan (Evan Vaughan) of Pengwern, Llangollen, married Angharad the daughter and sole heiress of Hywel (Howel) son of Tudur ap Ithel Fychan, thus gaining the lands of Mostyn Hall. This was followed by a further inheritance through a female line in about 1458 when their son Howel married Margaret the sole heiress of Gruffydd ap Rhys of Gloddaeth, thus establishing the connection with the Llandudno area. (A few years earlier, in 1448, the plague had been rampant, carrying off seven of Gruffydd's children in one week and leaving only Margaret.)

Margaret was kin to Henry, Earl of Richmond (later Henry VII), his father Edmund Tudur being her second cousin. She was the subject of a Welsh poem written about 1480 in which this kinship is referred to, but perhaps of more interest to us is the reference also made in the same poem to "Margaret of Gloddaeth" reclaiming land from the sea, which had yielded fine crops. The phrase that she "wouldest plough to Ireland along the land (coast) towards her" is perhaps suggestive of this activity being on the western side of the Morfa Rhianedd, and there are of course references and evidence from other sources of the changing North Wales coastline. One need only consider the now slight remains of Gogarth Abbey to see the possibilities.

In later life, Margaret made a second marriage to Henry Salusbury who himself held the Lordship of Mostyn (as distinct from the land upon which Mostyn Hall stands) from 1473 to 1501. It was, however, Howel and Margaret's son Richard (who had married Henry Salusbury's sister) who inherited the estates of Mostyn, Pengwern and Gloddaeth, and who also in 1501 obtained the grant of the vill (or Manor) of Mostyn. Richard's possessions also included two estates in Mon (Anglesey), which were part of the Pengwern inheritance.

Richard was a supporter of Henry, Earl of Richmond, and it has been recorded[3] that at Bosworth Field he commanded a force of 1,600 Flintshire miners and colliers, well equipped for battle. Though later pressed to follow Henry to court, he preferred to remain in Wales and in his later years was the sinecure Rector of Whitford, in which parish Mostyn is situated. He is

1 Burke's Peerage and Baronetage.

2 The Mostyns of Mostyn by The Rt.Hon.Lord Mostyn, D.L., F.S.A. and T.A.Glenn. London. Harrison and Sons Ltd. 1925.

3 Henry Taylor, M.A., F.S.A. Historian of Flint and District.

said to have "abjured Papal Supremacy" in 1535 and died at Mostyn Hall in February 1539.

The line continues with Thomas ap Richard who was the first to use the surname of Mostyn, soon after his father's death. He followed the family tradition in his patronage of the bards, and was esteemed by them for his interest in Welsh Literature. There are poems addressed to him during his lifetime and others written after his death. One elegy, by the bard Simwnt Vychan states that "Gloddaeth has become empty to us" and also has reference to the "free hawk of Creuddyn". (The Peregrine Falcon of the Great Orme).

Whilst it is thus probable that Thomas spent much time at Gloddaeth, he died at Mostyn in 1558, aged about 75 years. However, his wife Sian (Jane) who died in 1571, is buried at Llanrhos, in which parish Gloddaeth is situated. A 'marwnad' (elegy) to her begins as follows:- "Throughout the halls there is a cry: an hour is the short year because of the death of Sian Mostyn..... A warm hearted woman... She was buried in the chancel of Rhos, the true north of Medrod, and was put in the grave of Maelgwyn Gwynedd"[4].

Thomas and Sian had a large family of eight sons and five daughters. The oldest son was William ('Valiant William'), who in early life was a professional soldier, serving with distinction at the time of Wyatt's rebellion in January and February 1553/4. Shortly afterwards in March 1553/4 he was returned to Parliament and he was three times Sheriff for the County of Flint and once for Carnarvon. His interest in the Llandudno area is evidenced by the existence of a document dated 28th.February 1570/1, in which Nicholas, Bishop of Bangor granted him the right to take all gulls, hawks, wild fowl and rabbits within the Lordship of Creuthyne, excepting only wild swans. This grant was made for a term of 21 years at a rental of eight pence per year.[5] He died in 1576 and is buried at Whitford, his heir being his son Thomas. His original will is the earliest of those which are in the safe keeping of the Clwyd Record Office[6], dated 1566.

For the purposes for which this book is written, it is also of relevance to note the second son of Thomas and Sian. He was known as Richard of Bodysgallen and was reputedly a man of great learning. It seems probable that the Bodysgallen lands originally formed part of the Gloddaeth estate and were settled on Richard by his father Thomas. The Manor rights, however, belonged to the Crown and in 1545/6 these were granted for 21 years to a certain Lewis ap David Lloyd, gentleman. The lease was then assigned to William Mostyn of Mostyn (Richard's older brother) in 1557 and subsequently acquired in perpetuity.

Our particular interest in Richard lies in the fact that his daughter – and sole heiress – Margaret married Hugh Wynn some time before 1594. The Wynns of Bodysgallen were then in residence near to Llandudno for six generations, until Margaret Wynn (yet another sole heiress) married the fifth Mostyn Baronet, Sir Roger Mostyn, in 1766, thus returning the lands to the Mostyn Family.

4 Maelgwyn was King of Venedotia, or Gwynedd, in the sixth century. According to tradition he took refuge in Eglwys Rhos (Llanrhos Church) to escape the yellow plague; but looking from the church door observed a strange creature coming from the adjacent marsh and died, as had been prophesied. He was buried in the chancel.

5 Clwyd Record Office. Mostyn MSS.No.7079.

6 Clwyd Record office. Mostyn MSS.No.3724.

Thomas Mostyn, the son of William, enjoyed a long and active life, having first been trained to arms, as was his father. For a short time he also was a Member of Parliament and he was at various times Sheriff and a Justice of the Peace for the Counties of Anglesey, Flint and Carnarvon. He was knighted in 1599 and served on several commissions.

This was the age of the first Queen Elizabeth, a time when the gentry of Wales and England were much more at ease with each other than formerly. Thomas was a friend of many notables, including Burghley, Grey and Essex and he remained true to the traditional hospitality of the Welsh gentry, so that Mostyn Hall became noted for this.

Sir Thomas Mostyn seems to have been very fond of birds and the breeding of house doves at Gloddaeth dates from his time. He built the Gloddaeth dovecote and made other additions to the building. His doves may have been descended from the local rock pigeons for it seems there were problems with breeding in the dovecote, the birds preferring to quit at laying time for "the fastnesses of Ormeshead".[7]

Though the institution of household bards was now in slow decline, they were still present at Mostyn. One poem, by a kinsman Sion Tudur, is highly laudatory. This was written shortly after Thomas was knighted, one reference being to "the pinnacle and top of Gwynedd".

Sir Thomas took a personal interest in his tenants and could rightly be described as a reformer. He was among those who advocated the abolition of torture and the mitigation of the punishment for certain crimes. He died in 1617/18 and is buried at Whitford, being succeeded by his son Roger, who had been knighted only a few years after his father, in 1606.

Sir Roger Mostyn had married Mary, the eldest daughter of Sir John Wynn of Gwydir in 1596/7, and it is recorded in "The Mostyns of Mostyn" that he sometimes took the part of his father-in-law in the series of 'misunderstandings' which occurred between his father, Sir Thomas, and Sir John Wynn. It seems that in 1614 when Sir Thomas was still alive, the Wynns were able to assist in securing for Sir Roger the grant of the lordship of Mostyn together with the mining rights.

Sir Roger was a Sheriff of both Anglesey and Flint. He was a most notable public figure in Flintshire affairs and seems to have suffered some displeasure of the crown in King James's time, for his opposition to certain measures, including heavy taxation.

There are numerous documents and letters from this period which relate to Sir Roger and his father-in-law Sir John Wynn[8], and no doubt a detailed study of them would be of great interest. However, from the research that has already been done, this author is content to select a few details relevant to Llandudno. These include references to the poor state of the roads in the area, e.g. in 1624 it is very doubtful how they shall pass "from Glothaith to Gwydir". It is also evident that at that time the route from Mostyn to Gloddaeth was along the shore.[9] It also seems that Sir Roger had placed Gloddaeth at his

7 Letter XLIV of 'The Natural History of Selborne' by Gilbert White, 1760.

8 e.g. The Wynn Papers in The National Library of Wales.

9 For an interesting discussion concerning the vanished coast road, see Chapter XXII of 'The Evolution of a Coastline' by W.M.Ashton, published 1920 by Edward Stamford Ltd., Long Acre, WC2.

father-in-law's disposal as many of Sir John Wynn's letters are written from there.

Sir Roger Mostyn died in 1642 and, like his father, was buried at Whitford. His widow Mary died at Gloddaeth some years later in 1653. She, however, was buried at Gwydir Chapel, Llanrwst, and a letter of the time refers to Mostyn family members' intention to set out from Gloddaeth by 7 o'clock on Friday morning and to be at Gwydir within four or five hours.

It must be noted here that Sir Roger's heir was not his eldest son Thomas, for he had died in 1641, the year before his father's death.

This son Thomas, born about 1598, had himself been knighted in 1623, soon after his marriage to Elizabeth, the daughter of Sir James Whitelock who was Chief Justice of Chester. There is little to connect Sir Thomas with the Llandudno area, for he seems to have spent much time at Kilken (Cilcain) Hall and in London. After his death at a relatively early age, his widow married Owen Wynn, son of Sir John Wynn of Gwydir.

There were in fact less than ten months separating the deaths of Sir Thomas and his father Sir Roger but that had been sufficient time for the latter to add a codicil to his will. This provided that all bequests to the testator's son, Sir Thomas Mostyn, Knight, now deceased, would go to the latter's own son Roger Mostyn (the testator's grandson and now his heir).

Colonel Sir Roger Mostyn was born in 1623/4 and achieved distinction at an early age. He was a Royalist, present at the battle of Edgehill and involved in the siege of Flint Castle by the Commonwealth troops, after which an honourable surrender was made. He was fined for his activities and it was estimated that his Royalist support left him some £60,000 worse off,[10] much of this being due to his wartime expenditure including the feeding of the garrison and paying, clothing and equipping his troops.[11] It is said that in his later years he was worried due to the debts incurred during the Civil War but despite his financial problems he remained in command of the Flintshire Militia until his death, taking great pride in the efficiency of his own company.

After the restoration of the Monarchy, Colonel Mostyn was Knighted in June 1660 and, shortly afterwards, in August 1660 he was made a baronet. Whilst it is evident that much of the Colonel's life was centred on Mostyn, he was Sheriff of Carnarvon as well as of Flint and on occasions had residence at Gloddaeth as evidenced by letters written from there. His portrait, supposedly by Sir Peter Lely, has hung at Gloddaeth for many years.

Also of local interest is the account of the 'Progress' of the Duke of Beaufort (as Lord President) through North Wales in 1684, of which we read:- "Friday Iuly 25 his Grace the Duke of Beaufort parted from Mostyn extreamly well satisfied with the condition in which he found the *Militia of Flintshire*, and with his enterteinment: and taking the benefitt of a low tyde he progressed a great part of the way upon the sands, Sr Roger Mostyns Coach wth 6 horses also attending ye company towards the foot of Pen-men-maure Mountain, a dangerous precipice to ride in....... At night his Grace and Company arrived at Conwey".

10 An estimate made by his grandson, the 3rd.Baronet.

11 In passing it may be noted that there were four guns from the Civil War at Mostyn Hall. In 1925 it was written that 'one of these guns is said to have exploded during a coming of age celebration quite recently'.

Sir Roger died in October 1690 and like his forebears was buried at Whitford. He had married three times and the heir to the Baronetcy was his elder son Thomas, by his second marriage. (It will no doubt have been noted by the reader that throughout the period covered by this chapter there are the alternating names of Thomas and Roger).

Sir Thomas Mostyn, 2nd.Baronet, was born in 1651. He held high offices, being at various times the Deputy Lieutenant for Carnarvonshire and Sheriff for both that County and for Anglesey. He was four times returned as M.P. for Carnarvon and was a Commissioner of Taxes for Flintshire. A patron of the Arts, he much enlarged the Mostyn and Gloddaeth libraries and had a great interest in Welsh Literature as a collector of Welsh MSS.

Sir Thomas married Bridget, daughter of D'Arcy Savage in whose right he inherited several Manors and lands in Cheshire[12]. Of their eleven children all but three died young and there is in Llanrhos Church an inscription to Mary, a daughter who died in 1675. Until he succeeded his father he was known as "Mr.Mostyn of Gloddaeth", where he lived during his father's lifetime. Both he and his wife died at Gloddaeth in 1700, and he was the first of the Mostyn Baronets to be buried at Llanrhos Church.

The third Baronet, Sir Roger, was born in 1673 and was the eldest son of Sir Thomas. He was a Sheriff of Carnarvonshire and Constable of Flint Castle but was also notable as being an active Member of Parliament for more than thirty years. In 1703 he married Lady Essex Finch, the eldest daughter of the Earl of Winchelsea and Nottingham and a noted beauty of the day. He was known as a keen supporter of racing and often present at Newmarket. However, he lived much of the time at Gloddaeth and like his father he was buried at Llanrhos.

Sir Roger and Lady Essex had a large family and two of their younger sons achieved great distinction in the armed forces. These were the second son John,[13] who became a General and was also the Governor of Minorca, and the third son Savage[14] who became a Vice-Admiral and Controller of the Navy.

The eldest son Thomas was born in 1704. As a young man he travelled extensively being away for more than four years during which he visited most of the larger cities of Europe. He married Sarah, the daughter of Robert Western of London, and like others of his family was returned to Parliament on a number of occasions. He was a sitting member at the time of his death in 1758. Sir Thomas continued the family interest in the Arts, being a collector of rare and beautiful books and also of Roman busts.

An unexpected source of descriptive material concerning eighteenth century life is to be found in the British Medical Journal of 17th.November 1923. A paper entitled "An eighteenth Century Practitioner's Ledger" gives details of the lucrative practice of a Mr.William Coyne of Holywell. The ledger covers some twenty eight years from early 1746 to end 1773 during which

12 Included were the Manors of Beeston, Peckforton, Leighton, Thornton and Great Neston.

13 General John Mostyn's distinguished army career spanned more than forty years during the reigns of George II and George III. He is mentioned as being brilliantly witty, genial, good-humoured and gallant, as well as being universally popular both in the Army and at Court.

14 Vice-Admiral Savage Mostyn entered the Navy at an early age and saw early service in the West Indies and off the western coasts of Europe. He was an M.P. and for six years the Controller of the Navy. Later, with flag rank, he served as second-in-command of a fleet sent to North America.

it is evident that the main income of the practice arose from the treatment of members of the Mostyn family and household. The usual fee for a journey to Mostyn Hall was five shillings but it was one guinea for Gloddaeth. It is evident that both Sir Thomas and his successor made themselves responsible for the medical attendance to a very large number of people. These included the indoor servants, listed as housekeeper, cook, footmen, housemaids, laundrymaids, dairymaids, kitchenmaids and turnspits, together with the domestic chaplain, the steward and the nurse. The outdoor staff included gamekeepers, grooms, coachmen, ploughmen, postillions, cowmen, carters, husbandmen, poultrywomen and stableboys. Sir Thomas Mostyn also made himself responsible for Mr.Wynne, the then Estate Agent, and a great number of old retainers and poor persons.

Of the children of Sir Thomas and Lady Sarah, in addition to the heir we may note a younger son, Thomas Mostyn who was Rector of Christleton and is buried at Llanrhos. Also a daughter Anne, who in 1777 married Thomas Pennant of Downing, a notable naturalist and historian.

The fifth Baronet, Sir Roger Mostyn, was born in 1734 and married Margaret Wynn in 1766. It has already been noted in the chapter on "The Early Mostyns" that a consequence of this marriage was the return of Bodysgallen and its lands to the Mostyn family, for although she was the daughter of the Rev.Dr.Hugh Wynn she was the heiress of Robert Wynn of Bodysgallen.

Sir Roger, like so many of his family, was an M.P. for many years (over eight successive parliaments), a Lord Lieutenant of the County of Flint and a Colonel of the Flintshire Militia. He also shared the family interest in Welsh literature. He had a large family, of which more will be written in the next chapter, but only one son, who succeeded him in 1796 as the sixth Baronet.

Sir Thomas Mostyn, the sixth – and last – Baronet, was born in 1776. He was a great sportsman and driver of four in hand, and had a lifelong passion for hunting, particularly in the Bicester countryside. In a contemporary reference[15] he is described as "... a single man, possessed of a fine fortune, and at ease in the circumstances, the expense (of hunting) is not an object to him." Reference is also made to his kennels and the fact that many of the puppies had been 'walked' by his Welsh tenants, but it seems more likely that this would have been on the Flintshire and Cheshire estates than at Gloddaeth.

It is recorded that Sir Thomas divided his time between three locations. These were his London house, his seat in Wales and his residence near Bicester, where he spent the winter, in close proximity to his brother-in-law, Sir Edward Lloyd (later the first Lord Mostyn) who lived at Stratton Audley. The Rev.Griff Lloyd, who was a brother of Sir Edward Lloyd, was also a huntsman and was a friend of Sir Thomas, who had given him the living of Christleton parish near Chester, on condition that he kept a Curate. This Griff Lloyd, to whom reference will again be made later in this book, is recorded as being quite capable of travelling by Coach and Chaise from Cheshire for midnight arrival at Bicester, followed by a 4 a.m. rising for the day's hunting with return to Cheshire as an outside passenger the same night.

15 Written by 'Nimrod', a sporting correspondent of the time (1821).

Sir Thomas died in 1831 having been Member of Parliament for Flintshire for the whole of his adult life. He was also Sheriff of both Carnarvonshire and Merionethshire. He is buried at Llanrhos (see figure 1).

With the death of Sir Thomas, the male line of succession for the Mostyn family was ended. The continuation of the Mostyn name, through the inheritance of his sister and his brother- in-law, is the subject of the next chapter of this book.

Figure 1·
Llanrhos Church, near Llandudno
(Eglwys Rhos)

Reference has already been made in "The Early Mostyns" to the history of the Mostyn Family which was written in 1925 by the 3rd.Lord Mostyn. Whilst this is in itself excellent, it does, however, have one drawback, in that it covers only the period prior to 1831. The resort of Llandudno that we know today had, of course, not even been thought about at that time.

It is of some interest to speculate as to why the 3rd.Baron did not continue his account into the twentieth century. It may be that he considered the period from 1831 as being quite recent, known to members of the family and not yet worthy of an historical treatment. However, it may also be that it was convenient to stop at that point in time because of the break in the male line of succession which then occurred, for after 1831 the Mostyn name was continued by Sir Edward Price Lloyd who married one of Sir Thomas Mostyn's sisters.

It will again be useful to make reference to the appendices of this book. Appendix 3 shows the children of the 5th.Baronet, of whom six were girls. Three of them married and it was the husband of Elizabeth, the third daughter, who was created Baron Mostyn after the death of the sixth Baronet, Sir Thomas Mostyn, in 1831. This first Baron Mostyn, previously Sir Edward Pryce Lloyd, had succeeded his childless great uncle (the first Baronet Lloyd) in 1795, because of the earlier death of his father, Bell Lloyd. This latter relationship can be plainly seen in Appendix 4 in which also will be seen the already mentioned relationship of Sir Thomas Mostyn to his friend and fellow huntsman, the Reverend Griffith Lloyd.

Whilst this immediately previous paragraph can be regarded as an adequate description of the actualities of the Lloyd succession, it is rewarding to study the wills of the time and to note the extreme care with which they were drafted. The complex repetition of legalistic phrases in these lengthy documents is designed to cover all possible eventualities of family, whilst at the same time preserving the entail of estates with adherence to the principle of 'tail male' (i.e. inheritance through the male line) wherever possible.

An example is the will of the fifth Baronet, Sir Roger Mostyn, dated 11th.April 1793,[16] in which the possibility of his estates coming "into the possession of any one of my daughters or her issue male in failure of issue of my son" is fully considered. Also, in the will of Sir Roger's son, the sixth Baronet Sir Thomas Mostyn, dated 8th.June 1818,[17] the tail mail principle is again stated at length and it is by then apparent that the continuing line of inheritance is expected to be through "my nephew Edward Mostyn Lloyd, eldest son of my sister Dame Elizabeth Lloyd by Sir Edward Pryce Lloyd". Both wills are also very clear in their requirement that the name of Mostyn must be taken.

Another matter which is common to both wills, is of relevance to the Llandudno area, for it concerns Bodysgallen. In Sir Roger's will he requests his son to allow any of his unmarried daughters to reside at "Bodyscallan" as their country residence, rent free, if they should so desire. In its turn, Sir Thomas's will also specified the right of his unmarried sisters to reside free at Bodyscallan, and both Catherine and Mary Bridget Mostyn did in fact do so.

16 Clwyd Record Office. Mostyn MSS.No.3832.
17 Clwyd Record Office. Mostyn MSS.No.3870.

Sir Thomas died unmarried in 1831. By this time his eldest sister Essex was already dead, the next sister Charlotte was without issue and the way was thus cleared for the succession to continue through his third sister's marriage to Sir Edward Pryce Lloyd, for there were two sons of this marriage. In the interim, however, there was the matter of life tenure of the estates, which would be held first by Charlotte and then by Elizabeth, before passing on down the male line.

It has already been noted that Sir Thomas Mostyn's considerable expenditure as an ardent supporter of the hunt had received admiring comment from a contemporary writer; also, his three major establishments at Mostyn, Bicester and in London were doubtless maintained to the high standards usual for a free spending aristocracy in the Regency Period. There can be no doubt that there was an imbalance between Sir Thomas's income and his expenditure, and this is clearly shown by the existence of an 1818 agreement[18] with Messrs Coutts for a £100,000 mortgage at 5% for "divers manors in Flint, Merioneth and Carnarvon counties". Whilst this is an enormous sum for that time it must be noted that the manors concerned were stated to produce a net income of some £9,600 per annum.

Some years later, in 1829, the mortgage was for £120,000 and was then with the Law Life Insurance Company.[19] By 1830, the terms had been modified to allow for staged repayments of the capital sum[20] and the mortgage related specifically to the properties of Corsegedol, Plas Hen and Caerwys, the first two named being the very estates from which Sir Thomas in his will had directed the payment of certain large bequests.

With the death of Sir Thomas in 1831 there was then a complex interaction of his own will and that of his father Sir Roger, who had died 36 years earlier. For the major heirs the Mostyn surname was of course needed, for we have in Sir Roger's will that "each and every of my daughters and their issue when and as they shall respectively come into possession of the Estates hereby devised shall from henceforth and at all times thereafter take and use the Surname and Arms of Mostyn"; also in Sir Thomas's will it is stated that "all must take the name of Mostyn otherwise the estate is forfeited and it passes to the next in remainder".

At this time there were five of Sir Thomas's six sisters still living. Of these the oldest was Charlotte, now aged 63 years. She had married in 1792, before the making of her father's will, and her husband, Sir Thomas Swymmer Champneys of Orchardleigh, Somerset, was one of the named executors. Though childless, Charlotte would now have life tenure of the estates and after 1831 all documents refer to Sir Thomas Swymmer Mostyn Champneys and Dame Charlotte Margaret Mostyn Champneys. At this time, however, the circumstances of the Mostyn Champneys were complicated by the fact that from October 1827 Sir Thomas Swymmer Champneys had been an "insolvent debtor" and his own estate and effects were subject to the Court's assignee, a Samuel Sturgis.

The next of Sir Thomas's sisters was Elizabeth, then aged 55, who had married Edward Pryce Lloyd (later Sir Edward Pryce Lloyd) in 1794. As all concerned realised, the line would evidently continue in male succession through her elder son, Edward Mostyn Lloyd. In accord with the need for the Mostyn name, Sir Edward was created Baron Mostyn in September 1831[21] though it was a little earlier, in May 1831,[22] that the London Gazette had published the Royal Licence which was granted to Edward Mostyn Lloyd, of Mo-

18 Clwyd Record Office. Mostyn MSS Nos.4117 and 4211.
19 Clwyd Record Office. Mostyn MSS.No.3417.
20 Clwyd Record Office. Mostyn MSS.No.3418.
21 Clwyd Record Office. Mostyn MSS.No.7158.
22 Bangor University. Mostyn MSS.No.572.

styn Hall, Esquire, which allowed him to assume the name and arms of Mostyn (see figure 2).

> *Whitehall, May 7, 1831.*
>
> The King has been pleased to give and grant unto Edward-Mostyn Lloyd, of Mostyn-hall, in the county of Flint, Esq. eldest son of Sir Edward Pryce Lloyd, of Pengwern, in the same county, Bart. by Elizabeth his wife, daughter of Sir Roger Mostyn, late of Mostyn-hall aforesaid, Bart. deceased, and sister of Sir Thomas Mostyn, late of the same place, Bart. also deceased, His royal licence and authority that he and his issue may, in compliance with a clause contained in the last will and testament of his maternal uncle, the said Sir Thomas Mostyn, Bart. take and henceforth use the surname of Mostyn, in addition to and after that of Lloyd, and bear the arms of Mostyn quarterly with those of Lloyd, Mostyn in the first quarter such arms being first duly exemplified according to the laws of arms, and recorded in the Heralds' Office, otherwise the said licence and permission to be void and of none effect:
>
> And also to command, that the said royal concession and declaration be recorded in His Majesty's College of Arms.

Figure 2
An announcement in the London Gazette

Of Sir Thomas's three younger sisters, Anna Maria was married to Sir Robert Vaughan and was unlikely to be concerned with the succession, as also were the two spinster sisters, Catherine Mostyn and Mary Bridget Mostyn. There were thus no further name changes needed.

In 1832 Lord Mostyn and his family were in residence at Mostyn, and Sir Thomas and Dame Charlotte Mostyn Champneys spent time both in Somerset and in the Llandudno area. However, the Champneys activities at Gloddaeth were not to the Mostyn's liking for on 16th.February a complaint was made against them in Chancery by Lord and Lady Mostyn and the Hon.Edward Mostyn Lloyd Mostyn.[23] After reciting detail of Sir Roger Mostyn's will and establishing the fact that Edward Mostyn Lloyd Mostyn was entitled to the first estate of inheritance after the holding of the estate for life by both Dame Charlotte and by Elizabeth Lady Mostyn, the injunction from the Lord High Chancellor restrained the Mostyn Champneys from any further cutting of the oak, ash, beech, elm and other trees around the walks which "had been laid out with great taste and considerable expense at Gloddaeth" (see figure 3).

The injunction had followed a visit to Gloddaeth on the 6th.February by a Land Surveyor, at Lord Mostyn's instigation. This surveyor had observed the cutting and felling which was taking place[24] and had been informed by an agent, John Williams, (of whom much more will be written later in this book), that a considerable amount of further felling was planned for that Spring. The injunction was recorded as having been served on the same day (February 20th.) to Dame Charlotte at Bodysgallen, the Agent George Badcock and his Assistant Mr.John Williams in their house at Bodafon, and on Sir Thomas Mostyn Champneys at Orchardleigh Park in Somerset. The injunction was again served on 13th.May 1832, this time to three labourers in Gloddaeth Wood, the same Agent and his Assistant, and three other named persons including a joiner and a sawyer.

In August of this same year of 1832 Lord and Lady Mostyn were again the plaintiffs in another case with Sir Thomas and Dame Charlotte Mostyn Champneys among the defendants.[25] This case appears to have been the direct result of competing provisions of the wills of Sir Roger Mostyn and Sir Thomas Mostyn, relating to the estates of Corsegedol and

23 Clwyd Record Office. Mostyn MSS.No.4118.
24 Bangor University. Mostyn MSS.No.1160.
25 Clwyd Record Office. Mostyn MSS.No.4119.

Plas Hen, to which reference has already been made. These estates had come into Sir Roger's possession in the right of his wife, Dame Margaret Mostyn, through the will of her uncle, Evan Lloyd Vaughan. In Sir Roger's will (which is of course again recited at length in the document relating to the case) he had referred to the possibility of his estates coming into the possession of any one of his daughters, and he had directed that if this should be so, his trustees should pay to each other daughter

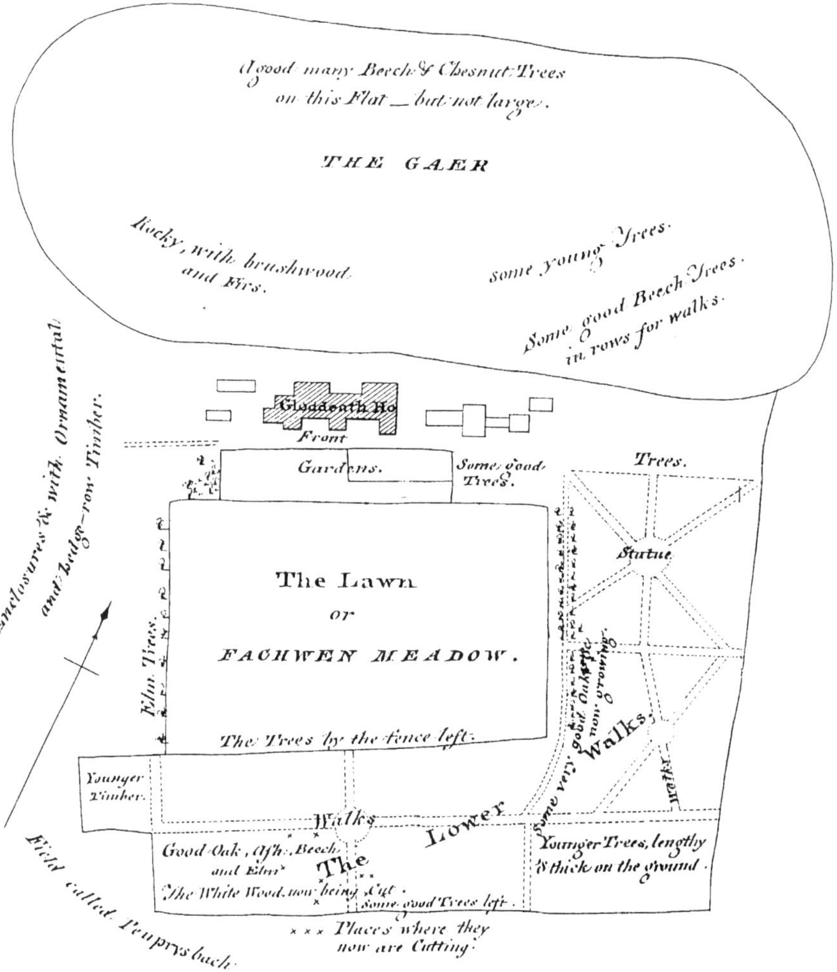

Figure 3

Part copy of a map exhibited by the complainants and referred to in the affidavits by Lord Mostyn and the Honorable Edward Mostyn Lloyd Mostyn which were sworn on the thirtieth day of April one thousand eight hundred and thirty two before Richard Humphreys, a Master in Chancery.

then living the sum of £10,000, unless the estate of his late wife's uncle was also held. In Sir Thomas's will (also again recited) the rents and profits of the Vaughan estates had been passed directly to Edward Mostyn Lloyd (now Edward Mostyn Lloyd Mostyn). It was the contention of Lord and Lady Mostyn that as Dame Charlotte Mostyn Champneys now had life interest in Sir Roger's own estates, the sums of £10,000 should be raised and paid to each other sister, including Lady Mostyn herself. The defendants, including Sir Thomas Swymmer Mostyn Champneys, who was now the sole survivor of the original trustees of Sir Roger's will, did not agree, contending that Dame Elizabeth should not have the £10,000 because of her son's direct interest in the Vaughan estates.

The recorded outcome of this hearing in Chancery was that all four of Dame Charlotte Mostyn Champneys sisters were entitled to have the sum of £10,000 raised and paid out of the estates, and that all necessary acts should be done by the surviving trustee, Sir Thomas Swymmer Mostyn Champneys. Indentures recording this judgement are dated 7th.August 1832 and are referred to in the copy receipts later signed by Lord and Lady Mostyn, Catherine Mostyn and Mary Bridget Mostyn.[26] In the case of Anna Maria, Lady Vaughan, a later document has been noted in which she and her husband acknowledged that they had no claim or demand upon the estates of Sir Roger Mostyn[27] and it may thus be inferred that she did also benefit from the judgement.

Whilst the result of this last mentioned hearing can in some respects be regarded as having clarified a rather confused situation, it was by no means the end of litigation. In January 1835 a bill of complaint was filed against Sir Thomas and Dame Charlotte Mostyn Champneys (and Samuel Sturgis, the Court's administrator for their Orchardleigh estate) by Lord and Lady Mostyn and the Hon.Edward Mostyn Lloyd Mostyn. The latter were described as being next entitled under Sir Roger Mostyn's will and in remainder expectant on the death of Dame Charlotte and the failure of her issue male.

The complaint related to the Lordship, Manor and lands of Gogarth, which had for many years been leased by the Mostyns from the Lord Bishop of Bangor.[28] It appears that the Mostyns sought a renewal of the lease, with different named lessees, and claimed that the defendants were bound to contribute to the expenses involved and to concur in all acts necessary for the renewal.

A supplementary bill of complaint relating to the same matter was filed in April of the next year, but by that time the affairs of the Mostyn Champneys had been further complicated by Sir Thomas being declared an insolvent debtor for the second time. In this case the Court appointed John Thomas Robinson and Jonathan Gillett as administrators and they were later to replace the previously appointed Samuel Sturgis in all matters related to the Orchardleigh estate.

The complications inherent in this uneasy situation were still not complete, for in March 1836 Samuel Sturgis had filed his own bill of complaint against Sir Thomas and Dame Charlotte Mostyn Champneys and in August of the same year the Vice-Chancellor made an order "to appoint a proper person to be receiver of the rents,

26 Clwyd Record Office. Mostyn MSS.No.3429.
27 Clwyd Record Office. Mostyn MSS.No.4152.
28 Clwyd Record Office. Mostyn MSS Nos.2256-2262.

royalties and profits of the estates, manors and hereditaments devised by the will of Sir Roger Mostyn". The name of John Maughan was suggested and he was in appointment by November 1836, thus effectively replacing the role of Sir Thomas Mostyn Champneys, the sole surviving executor of Sir Roger Mostyn's will.

The account of the various actions just referred to, is to be found in a document[29] in which the events over a number of years are detailed. It goes on to refer to other matters pertaining to 1836, including existing estate mortgages, a counterclaim by Dame Charlotte Mostyn Champneys that she was entitled to retain portions of rents and profits still in her hands, and to a claim for dilapidations made by Lord and Lady Mostyn.

This last mentioned document is dated 13th.August 1838 and it was not until that year that the signs of a satisfactory settlement were to emerge. In July of 1838 the various administrators had been able to report that all of Sir Thomas Swymmer Mostyn Champneys debts relating to his first insolvency had been paid, with the exception of some few which had been in dispute. There was a sufficiency of cash and assets held by the Accountant General to enable this first insolvency to be discharged and Lord Mostyn was willing to assent to this, without prejudice to Dame Charlotte's claim. Lord Mostyn was also desirous of contracting for the purchase of the estate for the lifetime of Dame Charlotte Margaret Mostyn Champneys, and he had made certain financial proposals which were acceptable to those concerned. These would include the paying off of Sir Thomas Mostyn Champneys' debts and allow Dame Charlotte to lease Gloddaeth under trusteeship for her life at a peppercorn rent.

The title of this very lengthy document is: "Arrangement between Sir Thomas Swymmer and Lady Mostyn Champneys and his assignees in his 2nd.insolvency as to the payment of his debts and the sale of Her Ladyship's life interest in the manors and hereditaments devised by the will of Sir R.Mostyn Bart". The agreed arrangement did, however, also make reference to the need for a substitution of more simple modes of assurance concerning the entail of the estate – to require an estate in fee in lieu of the existing estate tail – and this was doubtless sought as a consequence of the recent problems encountered with the wills of the last two Baronets.

It was some 18 months later, in March 1840, that the general provisions of the arrangement became formalized as an agreement.[30] Dame Charlotte was now a widow, Sir Thomas Mostyn Champneys having died in November 1839. On his part, the Hon.Edward Mostyn Lloyd Mostyn agreed to pay Dame Charlotte the sum of £10,000 within 3 months and to enter into a bond to secure it; to pay all her debts and to settle the case Sturgis v Champneys; to abandon all bills and proceedings of Lord Mostyn against the late Sir Thomas Mostyn Champneys; to settle certain financial matters relating to the Champneys Orchardleigh estate and to indemnify her from both the mortgages on the Gloddaeth and Gogarth estates and the annuities which were still payable to the younger sisters Catherine and Mary Bridget. On her part, Dame Charlotte conveyed to him, for her lifetime, all estates excluding Gloddaeth and Gogarth and agreed to join in all acts necessary for

29 Clwyd Record Office. Mostyn MSS.No.3422.
30 Clwyd Record Office. Mostyn MSS.No.4120.

barring all estates tail whatsoever in all the real estates devised to her for life by Sir Roger Mostyn.

In its turn, this agreement led to a number of further important developments concerning the Mostyn possessions. The numerous records available indicate a complex pattern of assignments, grants, leases and releases in connection with the various estates, with changes also in the appointed trustees. It is apparent that the aim throughout is to give control to the Hon.Edward Mostyn Lloyd Mostyn, in a manner acceptable to the older members of the family. Thus by September 1840 Lord and Lady Mostyn have conveyed Lady Mostyn's expectant life interest to him ("in consideration of their natural love and affection"), the necessary releases of the estates have been completed by Dame Charlotte,[31 & 32] and the spinster sisters have released all estates other than Gop from any liability to their annuities.[33] The indenture dated 8th.September 1840[34] carries the title: "Release of the within mentioned Manors advowsons messuages farms lands tenements and Heredits in Cos Chester Flint Carnarvon and Denbigh and in the city of Chester devised by the will of Sir Roger Mostyn for conveying the fee simple therein to the Honble Mr.Mostyn and for converting the base fee of Mr.Mostyn in the same to a fee simple absolute and for barring all estates tail of Mr.Mostyn and all remainders in the same estates".

It appeared that the way was now finally clear for an attempt to bring order into the unsatisfactory situation which was present after Sir Thomas Mostyn's death. This was to be done by the introduction of a private Act of Parliament entitled "An act for vesting parts of the settled estates of the Honble Edward Mostyn Lloyd Mostyn of Mostyn in Co of Flint in Trustees, upon trust to sell, mortgage or exchange the same, and to lay out the monies to arise therefrom in the payment of Debts Charges and Mortgages upon or affecting the same, or other estates settled to the same uses, or in the purchase of other estates to be settled to the same uses and for other purposes". This Act[35] received Royal Assent on 30th.July 1842

In a ten page preamble the Act first recites the terms of the will of Sir Thomas Mostyn and then lists those persons named in the will who were then still living. It goes on to refer to the Testator's large indebtedness in mortgage bonds, speciality and simple contract debts, and to the fact that the Corsegedol and Plas Hen estates – which were by the will charged with payment of the debts, expenses, legacies and annuities – would not raise a sufficient sum to pay the said mortgage bonds which related to both these and a number of other estates. It was also noted that several debts and expenses attending the execution of the will had been paid by Edward Pryce Lord Mostyn out of his own moneys. Such matters were held to be prejudicial to Edward Mostyn Lloyd Mostyn and his infant sons, and because of the limitations of the Testator's will there was need for the Aid and Authority of Parliament.

The Act removed the limitations inherent in Sir Thomas's will for the various manors and lands which were listed. These were then vested in three named trustees

31 Clwyd Record Office. Mostyn MSS.No.3077.
32 Clwyd Record Office. Mostyn MSS.No.3078.
33 Clwyd Record Office. Mostyn MSS.No.3082.
34 As 31.
35 Clwyd Record Office. Mostyn MSS.No.3972.

of whom two were family members (Hon.Thomas Pryce Lloyd and Cynric Lloyd the younger, respectively the brother and cousin of Edward Mostyn Lloyd Mostyn), and one who was presumably a lawyer, he being John Hancock Hall of the Middle Temple. These trustees were given the power to sell or mortgage properties, with the listed estates being categorised into three schedules. The trustees were also empowered to exchange or even purchase lands which could be related to those estates which were listed in the third schedule. The schedules do not comprise a comprehensive list of all the Mostyn possessions and it is noteworthy that whilst Bodysgallen is among those listed, Gloddaeth is not.

All money received by the Trustees was to be paid into the Bank of England in the name of the Accountant General of the High Court of Chancery, where it would be used as follows: firstly to pay costs and charges in connection with the Act itself; secondly to pay any costs attending the sale mortgage or exchange which had been made. It could then be used in paying the debts, expenses, legacies and annuities of Sir Thomas Mostyn's will.

The generally unsatisfactory financial situation was no doubt also eased at this time by several releases from substantial legacies which had been bequeathed in Sir Thomas's will, including one for £10,000 by Rev.Gruffydd Lloyd,[36] and another for the same sum by the executors of the late Richard Parry[37] who had been an executor but who had died in 1834. In each of these releases there is reference to the inadequate funds in the personal estate and the Corsegedol and Plas Hen estates from which the legacies were supposed to have been paid. Release from another possible legacy to his now one surviving unmarried sister, Mary Bridget (Catherine having died in 1841), payable only if she should ever marry, is also recorded.[38] Documents are also to be found relating to the release of a further large legacy which had in the meantime been assigned to a third party.[39 & 40] As a result of these and the arrangements of the Parliamentary Act, much progress would then appear to have been made in the ordering of Sir Thomas Mostyn's will and estate. It has, however, been noted that as late as 1850 the executors of Sir Thomas Mostyn are still presenting a balance sheet showing an outstanding mortgage sum in excess of £18,000.[41]

This historical survey of the Mostyns and matters related to Llandudno is now close in time to the relevant Enclosure Act of July 1843, which is the subject of a later chapter. However, there are other documents dated for that same year which relate directly to the Llandudno area, and which provide valuable sources of information of the local estates at that time.

In February 1843 the then existing 1828 lease of the Manor of Gogarth was surrendered. With the consent of Lady Mostyn Champneys, a new lease was granted by the Lord Bishop of Bangor, this being for the lives of Edward Mostyn Lloyd Mostyn, aged 46 years (presumably an error, as Edward Mostyn was born in 1795), Thomas Pryce Lloyd aged 41 years, and

36 Clwyd Record Office. Mostyn MSS.No.3956.
37 Clwyd Record Office. Mostyn MSS.No.3957.
38 Clwyd Record Office. Mostyn MSS.No.3958.
39 Clwyd Record Office. Mostyn MSS.No.5711.
40 Clwyd Record Office. Mostyn MSS.No.5712.
41 Clwyd Record Office. Mostyn MSS.No.3305.

Thomas Edward Mostyn Lloyd, aged 12 years.[42]

Thus one of the disagreements of a few years earlier was resolved. The document itself is of further interest in that it names the various localities comprising the estate, within the commots of Crethyn and Isap.

A little later, in March 1843, some seven manors and estates (none of which had been involved in the private Act of Parliament of the previous year) were conveyed to Trustees[43] for securing mortgage debts and interest, with a receiver (a James Parke) being appointed for administration purposes. This would seem to be a further major action in the planned recovery process and strategy being undertaken by Edward Mostyn Lloyd Mostyn.

The mortgages involved in this trusteeship of 1843 were again very substantial. They were four in number, each being for the sum of £25,000 and associated with particular schedules of estates or properties. The sixth schedule is that for the Gloddaeth estate, and this, together with the Rhyd estate, constitutes the security for one of the four mortgages.[44] The schedule is of particular interest as it gives the full list of all tenants of the Gloddaeth Estate for the year of 1843, together with the rents payable, which amount in total to the sum of £1,261-13s-5d.

---

42 Clwyd Record Office. Mostyn MSS.No.4037.
43 Clwyd Record Office. Mostyn MSS.No.3089.
44 Clwyd Record Office. Mostyn MSS.No.2055.

For the Llandudno of two hundred years ago, there are few general descriptions to be found. The locality seems to have been of such little general interest as to warrant not even a mention in the diary kept by Dr.Johnson during his lengthy excursion through North Wales in 1774. Though he passed from Penmaen Rhos to Conway before proceeding on to Bangor and Caernarvon, and later returned by the same route, the small diversion necessary to visit the Creuddyn was not made, nor, apparently, even considered. [45]

By 1792, a few lines concerning Llandudno are to be found in a small volume described as a "Pocket Companion" for those who make the tour of Caernarvonshire.[46] After a reference to "the promontory of Ormshead, well known to navigators" we read that "Here formerly was a nunnery; and near Llandudno is a copper mine. On an eminence near Dinac, in this parish was a famous rocking stone, called in Welch, Maen Sigil or Cryd Tudno; that is Tudno's Cradle. The isthmus that joins this headland to Caernarvonshire is a narrow, rich level, celebrated for producing excellent wheat".

Whilst it seems probable that the farming comment referred mainly to the holdings well away from the village (e.g. Maes du and Cwm Howard), the old farm at Gogarth may well have also been included. The population of Llandudno village and its immediate neighbourhood at this time was perhaps between two and three hundred (see figure 4).

In any account of the history of Llandudno it is the 1840's that must be regarded as the starting point for the transition from remote village to elegant seaside resort. The catalyst was the 1843 Inclosure Act for the locality, which was to be followed by the allotment of the common land and its subsequent drainage and development for building.

In general terms the description of Llandudno at this time is well known. The parish was the northernmost of the three which made up the Creuddyn peninsula, the detached portion of Caernarvonshire to the east of the River Conwy. The village heart was located on the south eastern slopes of the Great Orme, gaining shelter from the heights of Pen y Dinas, site of an ancient hill fort. The community was Welsh speaking, numbering little more than a thousand, and the working activities were centred on mining, farming and fishing. The isolated village was largely self sufficient, for in addition to the lower lying farms there were fertile areas on the Orme, as well as grazing which was available both there and on the area between the two shores, known as the Morfa Isa. The latter was, however, of poor quality for it was marshy and ill drained. The mines were higher up on the Orme whilst to the south west, along the estuary shore, there were the mine washeries and then the sand hills leading on to Deganwy.

Though Llandudno was blessed with a generally mild and salubrious climate, the month of January 1839 had been notable for a storm of unusual force. This had destroyed the roof of the old parish church of St.Tudno, situated on the northern side of the Great Orme and at some considerable and inconvenient distance from the village. Though its location was undoubtedly a factor in the sparse church attendance of the

45 'A Diary of a Journey into North Wales in the year 1774' by Samuel Johnson LL.D. Edited by R.Duppa LL.B. Printed 1816 by J.Moyes of Hatton Garden for Robert Jennings, 2 Poultrey, London.

46 'Caernarvonshire. A sketch of its History, Antiquities, Mountains and Productions'. Author unknown but published for Debrett Piccadilly 1792.

time, another was the rise in allegiance to the non-conforming churches in the area, whose adherents were now in the majority. It was not surprising that the ecclesiastical authorities decided to abandon the old church and to erect a new one, nearer to the village and almost at the bottom of the slope of the Orme. What is more surprising is the speed with which the new St.George's church was erected, for it was consecrated on 13th.August 1840.

At this point of the narrative the author is well aware that he has added nothing to that which is already well known about Llandudno. However, it is hoped that the references to be made to information now available from Mostyn Estate documents will do so, by adding to the general knowledge of some of the inhabitants and their properties. A major source of information has been the 1843 schedule of properties on the Gloddaeth estate, which has already been referred to at the end of the last chapter,[47] whilst another has been the study of the leases granted by the Mostyn Champneys in the ten years prior to 1843.[48] At the same time the author has drawn on the fascinating writings of Thomas Rowlands whose memories of his youth were written down nearly fifty years later, and which provide much information of houses and their occupants,[49] at this time.

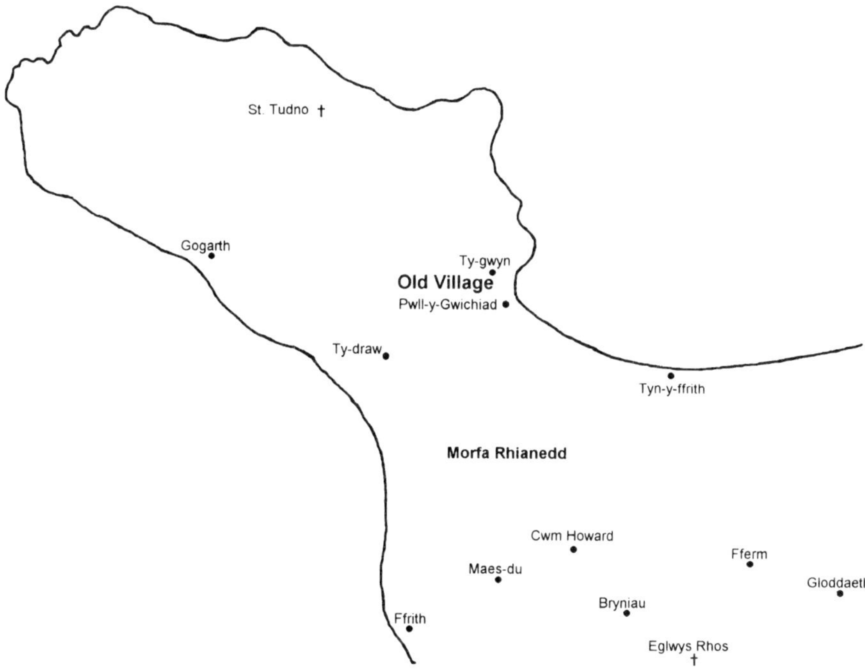

Figure 4
Creuddyn

47 Clwyd Record Office. Mostyn MSS.No.2055.
48 Clwyd Record Office. Mostyn MSS Nos.1009-1027 inclusive.
49 'Atgofion Hen Llandudno (Memories of Old Llandudno)' byThomas Rowlands, written about 1883.

Turning firstly to the farms around the perimeter of the Great Orme we may start with that of Gogarth, which was held in 1843 by Richard Jones, as a Mostyn tenant. This farm was let at an annual rental of £41-5s and its fields extended along the southern side of the Great Orme, where Llys Helig Drive is now to be found. Thomas Rowlands records how the old farmer would relate that in his own father's time, presumably about 1780, the ploughing had extended to the two large rocks now out in the sea,[50] and he comments on the considerable erosion that must have taken place.

Gogarth farm was situated just below the Gogarth spring which provided motive power for the 'Tom and Jerry' device which pumped water from the mines, and Rowlands also records that a Samuel Davies and his family lived nearby in a small cottage which was also named Tom and Jerry, after the machine.

The next farm is that of Ty Draw, on which site is now to be found the Loreto Convent. This was a larger farm, tenanted by David Jones at an annual rental of £65-14s-1d (see figure 5). His wife Margaret is praised by Rowlands, for 'there never was a more honest farmer's wife'.

A move north eastwards brings us to Pwll y Gwichiad, whose building was close to the site now occupied by Prince Edward Square. In 1843 this was tenanted by Elizabeth Jones and her rental of £35-8s-1d included an element for part of the Ty Gwyn land, the adjoining farm on which there had

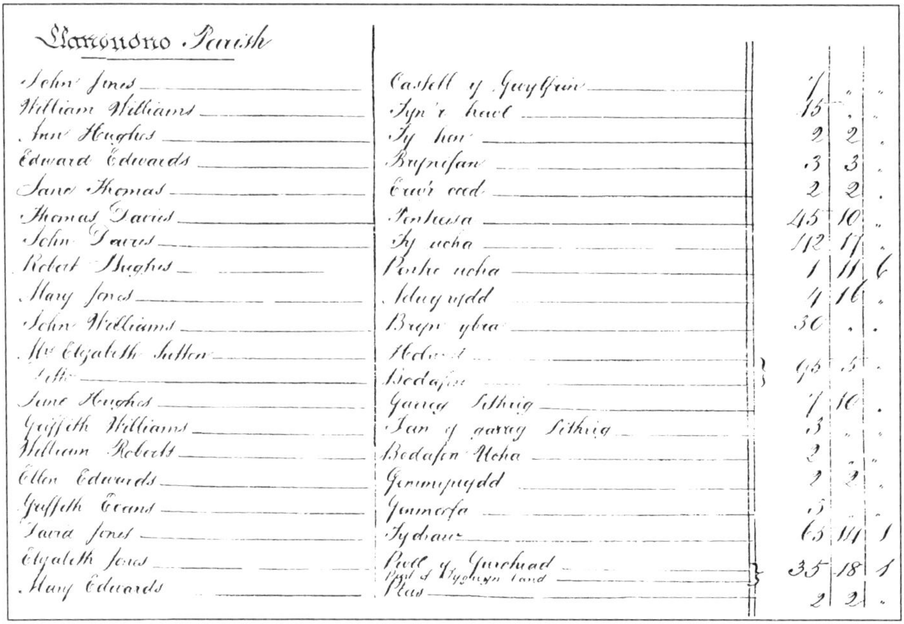

Llandudno Parish

Tenant	Property			
John Jones	Castell y Gwylfain	7	"	"
William Williams	Tyn'r heol	15	"	"
Ann Hughes	Ty hen	2	2	"
Edward Edwards	Brynifan	3	3	"
Jane Thomas	Erw'r eed	2	2	"
Thomas Davies	Penhesa	45	10	"
John Davies	Ty ucha	112	17	"
Robert Hughes	Perthi ucha	1	11	6
Mary Jones	Addwyfydd	4	16	"
John Williams	Bryn ybra	30	"	"
Mrs Elizabeth Sutton	Hebel	65	5	"
Ditto	Bodafon			
Jane Hughes	Gairay Sithig	7	10	"
Griffith Williams	Pen y garreg Sithig	3	"	"
William Roberts	Bodafon Ucha	2	"	"
Ellen Edwards	Gorrmynydd	2	2	"
Griffith Evans	Gwmerfa	5	"	"
David Jones	Ty draw	65	111	1
Elizabeth Jones	Pwll y Gwichiad Part of Tyglwyn land	35	18	1
Mary Edwards	Plas	2	2	"

Figure 5
Part of the 1843 schedule of Mostyn Properties

50 This is only one of the many references that the author has found relating to coast erosion.

been the chance discovery of surface copper ore, in 1835. It is evident that this farm had undergone some sub-division, for the schedule lists not only Edward Jones as paying a rental of £7-10s but also a Margaret Roberts whose rental was £4-2s-6d, also for a 'part of Ty Gwyn'. The Ty Gwyn Mining Company appears in the schedule as paying small rentals for 'Marian and other cottages' and for a 'garden by Ty Gwyn'. Edward Jones is described by Rowlands as being 'a remarkable man in many respects'.

Turning now to the farmlands upon the Orme itself, there are those of Pen y Mynydd Isaf and Pen y Mynydd Ucha, later to be known to many as Pink Farm and White Farm. They are respectively described by Rowlands as the homes of old Richard Davies and of Thomas Owen and his sons – one of whom (Edward) became the first butcher in the village. The Gloddaeth rental schedule clearly lists Richard Davies as the tenant of 'Penmynedd etc' for £18-15s, and the next entry, though being for Thomas Owen as expected, refers to the property of Tyddyn'rhendre, at £13-10s. At this time the author can only surmise that Tyddyn'rhendre and Pen y Mynydd Ucha may be one and the same.

It is fair to surmise that the rentals listed in the schedule will be related approximately to the size of the farm or smallholding and the rental for 'Wyddfryd', recorded as £7-10s seems in accord with this. The building itself is still to be seen, at the top of the present ski slope, and it has undergone recent restoration. In the 1840's it was the home of John and Betty Williams, who with their family are described as 'leading in every good establishment, both political and religious, especially the latter' (see figure 6).

Other properties upon the Great Orme whose larger rental schedules have been noted include those of Maes y facrell (£5, payable by Thomas Rogers and his wife Betty), Yr Off (probably Y Rofft) (£4-10s,

Robert Jones	Yr hen dafarn	5	.	.
Owen Jones	Yr Off	4	10	.
Thomas Rogers	Maes y facrell	5	.	.
George Williams	Tyn y fron	1	10	.
John Williams	Wyddfryd	7	10	.
Richard Davies	Penmynydd etc	18	15	.
Thomas Owen	Tyddyn'rhendre	13	10	
Richard Jones	Gogarth	41	5	.

Figure 6
Examples of entries on the 1843 schedule which are not readily capable of being photocopied.

payable by Owen Jones whose wife Nancy 'knew much of the old inhabitants') and Yr hen dafarn (£5, payable by Robert Jones, 'a teller of interesting tales').

The aforementioned correlations of properties in the Gloddaeth schedule with the memories of Thomas Rowlands are only a few of the many that can be made. A number of the entries show a rental of £1-1s (Croes Onen, George and Dragon, Cil y Llidiart) though that for Mrs.Ann Jones of Greenhill, who opened Llandudno's first Post Office in 1838, is £2-2s. The annual rentals for the Anabaptist and Wesleyan chapels (Tabernacl and Caersalem) were only 10s-6d (see figure 7). The 99 year lease for the latter is an unusual one, for most leases granted at this time were for only 60 years. It dates from May 1837[51] and was granted by Sir Thomas and Dame Charlotte Mostyn Champneys. The nine named Methodists to whom the lease was granted, included an engineer, a miner, an innkeeper, a shopkeeper and a miller. This list of trustees is headed by two named 'gentlemen' of Llandudno, these being John Jones and John Lester. The engineer was Joseph Tambling (or Tamblyn), of Cor-

51 Clwyd Record Office. Mostyn MSS.No.1023.

nish descent, who had arrived in Llandudno in 1834 and had quickly become a moving spirit of Methodism in the area. The building was later to become Dr.George Roberts's Grammar School, where William Morris Hughes, Australia's Prime Minister from 1916 to 1923, was educated in the 1870's.

As has already been noted, the memories of Thomas Rowlands were written many years after the events described. On the supporting evidence now found, it can be stated that they are remarkably accurate, though sometimes a little difficult to follow (at least in the English translation) as he wanders in retrospect over a route from Gogarth through Pen Morfa, Cwlach, Old Road, in various directions over the Great Orme and then down through the Llewelyn Avenue/Tudno Street area. His descriptions of local characters and their named homes are many in number and merit the further careful study which would be needed in order to relate the locations more precisely to the present day streets of Llandudno.

To illustrate further the wealth of information given, Rowlands notes that Owen Hughes, living in the present Tudno Street area, was the 'Captain of the Lady Champneys', and also recalls the account of old William Williams of Tai Newyddion for whom 'it was worth walking twenty miles to hear him say "Amen" – not a cold, lifeless and formal "Amen" but one that came from the depths of a broken heart and a tormented spirit'.

Atgofion Hen Llandudno is indeed a valuable social document, but one which must be read in the knowledge that its writer was a non-conformist, whose memories were written for his fellow dissenters, and which were somewhat selective. There is no mention of the public houses or their publicans, some of whom became entrepreneurs in the new Llandudno. Anglicans are similarly neglected, and there is, for example, no reference to the Worthingtons of Ty Glas, who were the lessees of the Old Mine. The new church receives only a passing mention, in that Rowlands states that the land in front of Cwlach Street was clear, with 'nothing to darken the horizon except St.George's Church'.

There is only one possible matter of fact noted by this author on which issue may be taken with Rowlands, this being concerned with the residence of Owen Owens and his wife Gwen, who are stated to have emigrated to America from Pendyffryn in Cwlach Street. The schedule of 1843 shows Owen Owens to be in Cwlach street but in Tan y Nant, and this is supported by the contract of 28 November 1835[52] in which a 60 year lease at £1-1s was granted, again by the Mostyn Champneys, to Owen Owens, miner, for a parcel of land called Tan y Nant on which building had already taken place.

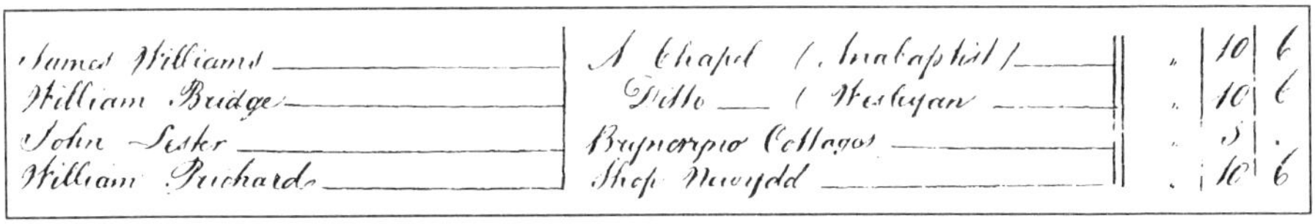

James Williams	A Chapel (Anabaptist)	.	10	6
William Bridge	Ditto (Wesleyan)	.	10	6
John Lister	Brynerypio Cottages	.	5	.
William Prichard	Shop Newydd	.	10	6

Figure 7

52 Clwyd Record Office. Mostyn MSS.No.1014.

Before moving on from pre-enclosure Llandudno, a little more can be added to the general scene of that time. Thomas Rowlands came to Llandudno as a small boy in the 1830's, and was soon to start work as a nine year old at 4d a day on the washing floors near Pen Morfa. He was one of many boys and girls employed and his description of the children chipping, hand-picking and washing the copper ore in order to obtain material for sending to the Amlwch or other smelters is indeed from another age. Prior to the construction of the Pen Morfa adit which was completed in 1842, ore was brought down from the old works by Dafydd Jones whose horses were harnessed to a cart drawing a sledge behind. Both were well loaded, with the sledge acting as a kind of brake. The completion of the drainage edit enabled the ore to be trammed out to Pen Morfa and the presence of the narrow gauge rails bringing ore from the mines conjures up an industrial scene that must be almost unbelievable to today's residents of that area. The Pen Morfa adit can still be seen, draining into the model yacht pond before overflowing to the sea.

The Morfa Isa, adjoining some of the lower farms already described, comprised the main part of the land between Llandudno's two shores. It was on this common area that, in winter, the animals from Ty Gwyn, Pwyll y gwichiad and smallholdings such as Ty'n pwll were turned out. These were mostly cattle but also included a few sheep. A notable feature must have been the rabbit warrens which were very numerous. The larger ones were shared or claimed between the various nearby cottages[53] and no doubt provided a welcome addition to the cottager's diet.

It would be wrong to conclude this picture of Llandudno in 1843 and leave an impression of no homes whatever other than on the Orme's slopes and the immediate vicinity. The Inclosure map of 1847 shows a surprising number of dwellings near to the shore line and the area which is now Mostyn Street. It is likely that many had been built on the common land in accordance with the Welsh custom of Hafod y nos (also seen as 'Hafod unos', 'ty unnos' and 'ty un nos') whereby title could be obtained if a dwelling was built overnight and a fire lit by morning. Though many of these dwellings may have been makeshift and primitive in character they are referred to by Thomas Rowlands as cottages and small houses, and he names a number of their occupants. It seems possible that the Ty'n pwll already referred to was one such home, for he locates it in the middle of what is now Gloddaeth Street.

On the subject of schools, Rowlands is again helpful. The first that he remembers is in a small schoolroom behind Croes Onen, and there is indeed a marking as such on the Inclosure map of 1847. As the teacher was said to be a Frenchman, a Mr.Louis, it is of interest to speculate upon the language of instruction! Rowlands avers that a Mary Ellen held another school in 'Hen Gapel Bach' and that before long a school was maintained by the Dissenters in the different chapels in turn. There is no reference to any schoolroom in Llandudno in the 1843 Gloddaeth Estate schedule though it was not long after, in November 1845, that the land of the St.George's National School was jointly conveyed by Dame Charlotte Mostyn Champneys and the Hon.Edward Mostyn Lloyd Mostyn to the Venerable Richard Newcombe and Rev.John Lloyd Williams.[54] As this pre-

53 'Cofiant y Diweddar William Pritchard, Llandudno (Biography of the late William Pritchard, Llandudno)
54 Information from the Mostyn Estate Office, Llandudno.

dates the Inclosure allotments, the school has been included on the map given.

The Llandudno Parish is of an unexpected shape, its boundary with Eglwys-rhos Parish moving to the shoreline before cutting back inland to include the areas of Bodafon, Bryn y bia and the Little Orme. The 1841 census identifies these two sections of the parish as being the Upper Township with 166 inhabited dwellings, and the Lower Township with 30 dwellings. For the latter portion the Gloddaeth schedule refers to a number of these, including the Little Orme farms of Pentre isa (Thomas Davies, rental £45-10s) and Ty Ucha (John Davies, rental £42-17s). A Mrs.Elizabeth Sutton held both Holand (on Bodafon Road) and Bodafon at £95-5s and close by was Adwy rydd (Mary Jones, rental £4-16s) and Bryn y bia (rented at £30 by John Williams the Mostyn agent, who was later to move to Bodafon).

Whilst still remaining with the Gloddaeth Rental Schedule, this chapter may conveniently be concluded by referring to some of the properties of the Manor of Gloddaeth which were located in the Eglwys Rhos Parish. There were fields and farms including Gloddaeth Isa (Mrs.Jane Evans, rental £51-15s), Maesdu (Joseph Hughes, rental £148-8s-9d) Brynia (divided between Thomas Jones, rental £51-18s-5d and Margaret Roberts, rental £9-4s) and Maes y Maenllwyd (divided between three tenants, Robert Jones, rental £43-5s-4d, Margaret Roberts, £26-1s-8d

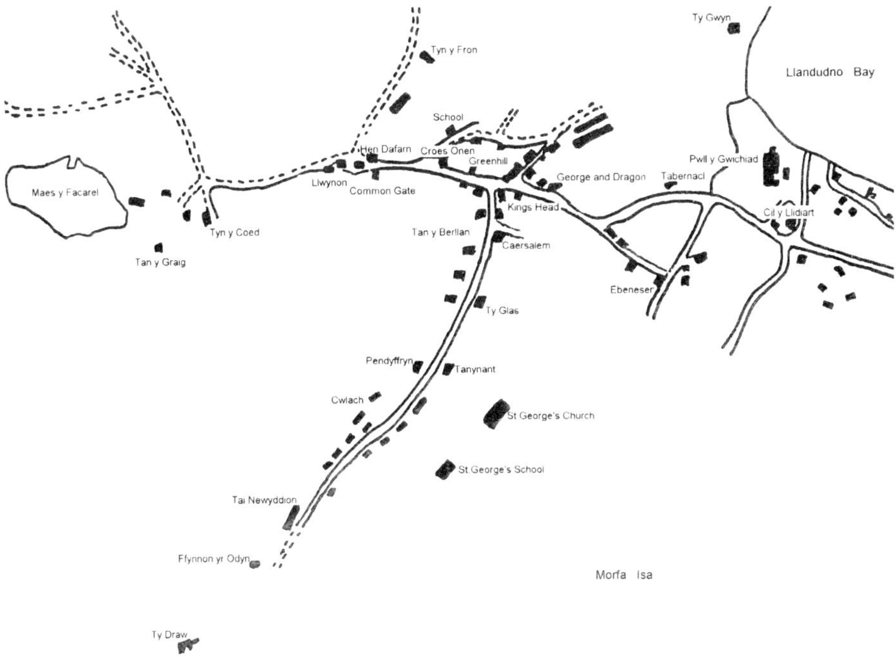

Figure 8
Llandudno Village
Based on Inclosure Map of 1847

and Thomas Jones, £6-18s-9d). The property of Tyn y ffrith (John Roberts, rental £4-10s) is also worthy of note.

Suggestions for General Reading

'Llandudno, Queen of the Welsh Resorts'
Ivor Wynne Jones. John Jones Cardiff Ltd. 1975

'Llandudno, A Pictorial History'
Richard Glynne Jones. Llandudno Town Council. 1985

'The Great Orme Copper Mines'
Don Smith. Creuddyn Publications. 1988

'Llandudno's Story'
Michael Senior. Gwasg Carreg Gwalch. 1986

'A History of the Parish Church of St.George and the growth of Llandudno'
Dr.B.G.Morgan.F.R.Hist.S. Colwyn Duplicating. n.d.

'St.Tudno and St.Tudno's Church. A Short History'
T. F. Wynne. Clwyd Press. n. d.

'Following the Footsteps of Thomas Rowlands'
D.J.Roberts. Llandudno & District Historical Society Information Sheet. 1990

'Ebeneser. A story of Llandudno and one of its Churches'
Rev.J.Roger Roberts. Photoprint Services, Conwy. 1975

The process of Enclosure (or Inclosure), whereby ownership of land became concentrated into fewer hands, had been slow but continual in England from the time of the Middle Ages. Its development was associated with the increasing need of production not merely for local subsistence, but for a larger market, as with, for example, the expanding textile industry of Tudor and Stuart times. Another factor which aided the process was that the Open Field System, whilst suited to the needs of a small community, was slow to respond to changes in agricultural methods, such as improved drainage systems and varied crop rotations.

Much of the early enclosure was effected by private arrangement, in those localities where this was practicable, and by the early eighteenth century the members of the nobility were mortgaging their estates at the prevailing low interest rates in order to buy more land. There was by that time the possible recourse to Parliamentary Powers, if necessary, by those who controlled the greater part of the land involved, but Enclosure by Act of Parliament was of little importance until after 1760. After that time, however, the enclosure process greatly accelerated and it has been estimated that between 1760 and 1844 there were some 4,000 relevant Acts of Parliament, most of these being concentrated in the two short periods of 1760 to 1780 and 1798 to 1815. These involved some six million acres of open field, common pasture and waste land.[55]

In Wales, the advent of Parliamentary Enclosure Acts enabled the process of enclosure – which had already been taking place in the peripheral lowlands – to move into the more inaccessible regions. It is recorded[56] that seventy six Acts of Parliament relating to Wales were introduced in the period 1801 to 1815, with lesser numbers in following years, up until the 1860's. However it does not seem probable that many of these were related to agricultural changes for in the words of the Land Report of 1896[57]:- "It would be idle to suppose that the main motive of the Welsh landowners who eagerly sought the facilities given by Parliament was to extend the margin of cultivation. They saw... that the movement gave them the opportunity of acquiring the sheepwalks and pasture lands till then unenclosed as their own in severalty under the title of an Act of Parliament, while the prospect of costs gave the family solicitors of the Principality a sufficient inducement to use their best endeavours to secure the passing of an Inclosure Act wherever a waste was extensive enough".

The introduction of Enclosure to Caernarvonshire, as in some parts of England, was not without violent incident.[58] The earliest Act for the County, in 1802, was that for the crown common of Rhoshirwaun, and involved land on which many had been allowed to squat over the years. They forcibly resisted attempts to displace them from their cottages and the act was not in final operation until 1814. A little later, following a similar Act benefitting the Vaynol Estate, the Riot Act was read at Llanddeiniolen and six rioters were arrested. The resentment was general, and, following other Acts, there was trouble to the west of Pwllheli and in areas from Nevin to Llanllyfni, because of the loss of the right of

55 'The Origins of Modern English Society' by Harold Perkin. Routledge and Kegan Paul. 1969.

56 'A History of Wales 1815-1906' by D.Gareth Evans. University of Wales Press. 1989.

57 'A History of Caernarvonshire' by A.H.Dodd. Published 1968 by Caernarvonshire Historical Society. Bridge Books Edition 1990.

58 As 57.

cutting turf ('turbary') and the displacement of cottagers who were said to have 'encroached' on the land. In one case only was an act defeated, this being the proposal in 1826 to enclose common lands of Llandwrog and Llanwnda, which would have included the village of Rhostryfan with its 140 houses.

The Inclosure act dated 12th.July 1843 for the parishes of Eglwysrhos, Llandudno and Llangwstenin is thus one of the later acts relating to North Wales. It was not the first one in the locality with which the Mostyn family had been involved for small allotments were received by Sir Edward Pryce Lloyd, later the first Lord Mostyn, under the Abergele Inclosure Act of 1826.[59] However, this 1843 Act was introduced to Parliament by one whose expectations of benefit would certainly have been high, for, as already explained, the Hon.E.M.Lloyd Mostyn, M.P., was now the major landowner in the area (see figure 9).

The printed Act[60] is a lengthy document of many paragraphs. Its general directives concerning the allotment of the land to be enclosed were, however, relatively simple. These only stipulated that a small allocation should be made to the inhabitants (in practice this was to the Churchwardens of the Parishes), that

ANNO SEXTO & SEPTIMO

VICTORIÆ REGINÆ.

Cap. 14.

An Act for inclosing Lands in the several Parishes of *Eglwys-rhos*, *Llandudno*, and *Llangwstenin* in the County of *Carnarvon*, and in the Parish of *Llandrillo* in the Counties of *Denbigh* and *Carnarvon*, or either of them.

[12th *July* 1843.]

WHEREAS there are within the several Parishes of *Eglwys-rhos*, *Llandudno*, and *Llangwstenin* in the County of *Carnarvon*, and in the Parish of *Llandrillo* in the Counties of *Denbigh* and *Carnarvon*, or either of them, divers Commons, Commonable Lands, and Waste Grounds, Heaths, Open and Common and other Fields and Waste Lands, and other Common Lands and Waste Grounds, which lie intermixed in small Parcels, and are inconveniently situated for the Use and Enjoyment of the several Proprietors thereof and other Parties interested therein, and in their present State are incapable of any considerable Improvements: And whereas the Right Reverend *Christopher* Lord Bishop of *Bangor*, in right of his Bishopric, is or claims to be Lord of the Manor of *Gogarth* in the said Parish of *Llandudno* t And whereas the said *Christopher* Lord Bishop of *Bangor*, in right of his See aforesaid, the Honourable *Edward Mostyn Lloyd Mostyn*, Sir *Richard Bulkeley Williams Bulkeley* Baronet, Dame *Margaret Mostyn Champneys* Widow, Dame *Silence Erskine* Widow, *Thomas Peers Williams* Esquire, *Lloyd Hesketh*

[*Private.*] 5 *d* *Bamford*

Figure 9

59 Bangor University. Mostyn MSS.No.255.

60 Clwyd Record Office. Mostyn MSS.No.3335.

an allocation should be made to the Lord of the Manor of Gogarth (i.e. the Bishop of Bangor) and that the Vicar of Llandrillo and the Perpetual Curates of Llandudno, Eglwysrhos and Llangwstenin should have their full equivalent of glebe lands and rights of common. For the residue it was directed that the "Commissioner shall adjudge".

The Commissioner appointed was a "Mr.Richard Yates of Whittington in the County of Salop, Gentleman". It is worthy of note that his judgements were not made in great haste, for they required a precise knowledge of the areas of land which were listed as comprising the "Homesteads Gardens Orchards and Ancient Enclosures" of the Parishes. The Commissioner's Maps were completed by 1847[61] and his allotments were made with the date of 25th.April 1848. There was also a supplemental award dated 24th.April 1849, but this was merely a technical clarification of the award, in which it was stated that the Hon.Edward Mostyn Lloyd Mostyn held Gloddaeth in fee simple but Bodysgallen as the tenant for life with remainder to his issue in tail in accordance with the will of the late Sir Thomas Mostyn, Baronet.

Before turning to the allotments actually made by the Commissioner it is of interest to note the extent of the then Gloddaeth Estate. Addition of his freeholdings and the land under lease from the Bishop shows that the Hon.Edward Mostyn Lloyd Mostyn was already the holder of nearly 750 of the 900 acres listed in the Commissioner's survey of the Llandudno Parish. (The Mostyn holdings in the other two parishes were not of such an overwhelming proportion, being respectively 1,478 of 3,026 acres in Eglwysrhos and 182 of 1,061 acres in Llangwstenin). As the enclosure allotment would obviously bear a relation to the extent of land already held, a large allocation was to be expected.

In Llandudno Parish large allotments of land on the Great Orme were made to the Hon.E.M.Lloyd Mostyn. These included parcels of 389 acres, 105 acres and 37 acres. Other allotments on the great Orme included 23 acres to Thomas Peers Williams of Marl, 14 acres to Sir R.B.W.Bulkeley and 45 acres to J.Lloyd Jones Esq, (these corresponding approximately to the extent of the farmland present today). Other allotments to the Hon.Lloyd Mostyn included large areas in the Bodafon region of the parish, and, crucially, some smaller areas along and inland from the north shore, now at the heart of modern Llandudno. In total the allotments to the Hon.Lloyd Mostyn amounted to no less than 832 acres of the 955 acres distributed by the Commissioner.

The Gloddaeth Estate, which at this time was already large and under the administration of a local agent for the Mostyn family, was thus greatly increased in size by enclosure. Much of the newly acquired land was contiguous to areas already owned, e.g. the north shore allotments were adjacent to the Mostyn owned farm of Pwll y Gwichiad. It seems that views were already developing concerning the convenience or possible potential use of the different pieces of land, for Richard Yates had already recorded an exchange of lands between the Hon.Lloyd Mostyn and Mr.William Jones (a holder of some of the 'Ancient Enclosed Land' on the Great Orme). In this exchange it seems that a small piece of land allotted to the latter near to the north shore was transferred in exchange for land near the old village.

61 Clwyd Record Office. Mostyn MSS.No.4707.

The Enclosure Map and Schedules for Llandudno are also quite specific in relation to the 'Particulars of Roads', giving details of them in two separate schedules, one relating to public carriageways and one to the private lands. Three Public Carriageways are specified as to be of breadth ten yards and the Bridle Road on 'Llandudno Mountain' (i.e. the Great Orme) had to be of six yards breadth.

The parish road to Conway at this time followed a route which today gives rise to surprise. In present day terms it passed through what is now North Parade then by Cil y Lidiart, near the present Carlton to Ty Isa Road. From thence it passed along Somerset Street into Bodafon Street, before turning left through Gloddaeth Crescent to the shore, along which it continued as far as Nant y Gamar Road. It then followed Nant y Gamar Road and Tan y Bryn to Llanrhos and thence to Conway.[62] The present, more direct, Conway Road to Llanrhos was not yet made (see figure 10).

Reference has been made in a previous chapter to the dwellings which had been established on the Morfa Isa, near to the north shoreline. It seems that the area was not level, as it is today, for we may read in Thomas Rowlands' Memories of those "living near the sand dunes where the Parade and Lloyd Street and part of Mostyn Street stand".[63] The preamble to the 1843 Act had referred to "divers commons, commonable lands and waster grounds.... in their present state incapable of considerable improvements" and in an article written in 1909[64] John Roberts described a "sandy, hilly expanse, similar to the West Shore". He states that one of these hills stood on the position of the St.George's Hotel, with a cottage erected on its slope. He names this cottage as Brynyfelin and hence opines that there had perhaps earlier been a mill on the site.

The Morfa Isa enclosure areas were thus concerned with land of very poor quality, upon which there were perhaps two dozen or so cottages, well away from the established village. To most observers there would seem at that time to be no great future for the area and little to suggest that the acquisition would be of significance to the Gloddaeth Estate and the Hon.Mostyn, particularly bearing in mind that the Enclosure Award specifically required the fencing of each piece of ground allotted.

How, then, did the idea of development of the area as a fashionable watering place come about? It is popularly supposed that this was entirely fortuitous, following a chance remark by a certain Owen Williams who visited the town in the interim between the Enclosure Act and the Allotment of the lands to be enclosed. The author, however, is forced to conclude that this is an oversimplification, to give a charming, though fanciful, story. There can, however, be no doubt that Owen Williams acted as the prime catalyst which was required to initiate the development proposals, but there had been others who had appreciated the beauty of the crescent bay and the magnificence of the local views. It is also noteworthy that from the earliest years of the nineteenth century there had been a general move by hard pressed landlords to search for sources of non-agricultural revenue from their estates.

62 A description of the route is given in the Llandudno Advertiser issue of 10th.January 1925, by the local historian John Roberts.

63 'Atgofion Hen Llandudno'. Thomas Rowlands.

64 Article in series 'Llandudno as it was' by John Roberts. Llandudno Advertiser issue of 3rd.April 1909.

An account of some early publicity for Llandudno is to be found in another of the John Roberts articles in the local newspaper.[65] it seems that a Mr.John Smith, who in 1823 was editor of the Liverpool Mercury, was given a glowing account of Llandudno by the Rev.Dr.Pritchard of Llangollen, who had been brought up in Llandudno and who had worked in the copper mines as a boy. After making his own visit to Llandudno, Mr.Smith wrote several pieces in his paper describing Llandudno as a suitable health resort and bathing place. John Roberts states that these attracted much notice, especially among the people of Lancashire, and that Smith's views were

Figure 10
The Nant y Gamar road to Conway is clearly shown on the first Ordnance Survey map, printed in the early 1840's.

65 Ibid. 29th.May 1909.

also brought to the attention of the Mostyns. It is certain that by the 1840's steam-boats were plying from Liverpool along the North Wales coast, bringing a handful of visitors to the village. One of these was the 'Cambria' and from this and other vessels the landing and embarkment of passengers was effected by the small boats of the enterprising locals. However, it seems that the accommodation available for visitors was very limited, being mainly provided by two small inns, even as late as 1849.[66]

The development of Llandudno as a resort was not, however, the only possibility that had been mooted. In 1836, with the formation of the St.George's Harbour Company, tnere were suggestions that Llandudno was a possible choice as the main port for crossing to Ireland, thus needing a railway connection. Though this scheme was overtaken by circumstances, with the choice in 1838 of Holyhead as the most suitable port position, the notion of a port lingered on for another twenty years and may have figured in the Mostyn thinking. It may also be noted that there had been earlier attempts in Wales by private landowners to develop complete towns on their estates, notably at Aberaeron, Milford Haven and Tremadoc, and it seems very unlikely that the Mostyns were unaware of these precedents.[67]

The evidence available would thus suggest that active consideration of the use of the newly acquired land – together with that which was already owned previously – was already being given by the Hon.E.M.Lloyd Mostyn when Mr.Owen Williams made his first visit to Llandudno, in the company of a friend who was attending a shareholder's meeting of a Llandudno mine. For a description of that visit and the subsequent events, we can do no better than to give Owen Williams's own words, written nearly forty years later.[68]

'We left Liverpool by the steamer and landed at Llandudno in a small boat. It was a beautiful summer's day, and Llandudno, so far as the natural beauties of the scenery were concerned, was most picturesque and striking. On landing on the beach the writer of this exclaimed "What a beautiful place this is, and what a fine watering place it would make!", adding that Providence had done His share in bringing into existence the splendid scenery, and it was now only necessary to find the man to do his part to make it a great resort and watering place. After the business of the mining meeting had been transacted the members dined at the public house on the side of the mountain and known as the King's Head. At the dinner table Mr.Jones (the friend) mentioned the suggestion I had made and I was a good deal teased for suggesting such a wild scheme. However, the subject soon gave place to other matters of conversation. For in a day or two afterwards, I received a letter from the then Honourable Mr.Mostyn, now Lord Mostyn, inviting me to meet him at Gloddaeth, near Llandudno. Not knowing that he was the owner of the property I could not think what he could want to see me about. Indeed, I thought the letter was intended for some other person. I replied, therefore, asking if the letter was for me and if it was, would he be so kind as to inform me of the nature of the business he wishes to see me upon. In reply, Mr.Mostyn informed me that his agent (the later Mr.John Williams of Bodafon) who was present at the dinner had mentioned to him the suggestion I had made with respect to Llandudno becom-

66 Article in Liverpool Mercury, issue of 22nd.May 1849.
67 'Settlement and Society in Wales'. Edited by D.Huw Owen. University of Wales Press. 1989.
68 'Llandudno News Sheet' dated 9th.August 1882. Copy in Estate Office.

ing a watering place, and that he wished to see me on that business.

I went over accordingly. On this occasion the weather was most unpropitious. The rain came down in torrents and the Hon.Mr.Mostyn, his agent and myself took possession of a very primitive sort of bathing box on the edge of the shore belonging to the late Mr.Wm.Jones, Bodhyfryd. In that box was our first meeting and conversation, and in it I received instructions to take a survey and report showing my views of the Llandudno of the future. I prepared a report, and Mr.Mostyn forwarded it to the architect of the estate in London for his opinion. The plan and report were returned to me approved by Mr.Mostyn without one alteration, and with an instruction to proceed with the work of bringing Llandudno into existence.'

The report and survey thus commissioned were to be of the utmost importance in the development of Llandudno, for they were to form the basis of the offer of land for sale by public auction which was to take place in August 1849.

As a consequence of the commission given to Owen Williams, a sale of building land by public auction was advertised to take place on Tuesday and Wednesday the 28th.and 29th.of August, 1849.[69] No fewer than 176 separate lots of land were listed, these being described as 'On the Estate of Gloddaeth belonging to the Honourable E.M.L.Mostyn,M.P.' The lots were stated as being suitable for mansions, family dwellings, villas and other residences.

The cover of the brochure of plans was in itself a short catalogue and guide to Llandudno's situation and attractiveness. Llandudno is stated to be pleasantly situated in a beautiful and romantic part of Wales, sheltered from the cold northerly and westerly winds and with a genial and delightful atmosphere at all times of the year, so that it may be referred to as the 'Italy of Wales'. There is mention of the Conway and Menai suspension and tubular bridges, those at Conway being stated as being in the immediate neighbourhood and those at Menai being within an hour and a half's sail. Powerful and swift steam vessels are stated to land and embark passengers every day in summer and four times weekly in winter whilst the Chester and Holyhead Railway is noted as being only four miles distant from the town, thus affording daily communication to all the principal towns and cities in the Kingdom (see figure 11).

The description is lyrical in its references to rich, wild and majestic mountain scenery, extensive views of land and water, and the salubrity of the district, all these being 'sure to draw together the lovers of nature, whether in pursuit of Health, Recreation or Retirement'. The pleasures of Boating, Fishing and Sea Bathing are described, the latter to be enjoyed 'without the slightest risk'. It is stated that already the demands for accommodation being made cannot be provided and that ere long Llandudno will become the most popular summer resort in Wales.

It is evident that Owen Williams, together with John Williams the local Mostyn Agent, had done a considerable amount of preparatory work prior to the auction. The land on offer is stated as having been thoroughly drained and carefully laid out, at considerable expense to the Proprietor. Also, and of great significance, it is stated that 'A series of Building Regulations have been fixed on, for the purpose of preserving the comfort of those who settle in the district, and ensuring proper ventilation, sewerage, drainage and propriety of Fronting and Elevation, so that *none shall suffer hereafter by the caprice or cupidity of others.*'

Examination of the four separately printed plans of different areas which are published in the prospectus shows an ambitious scheme involving some 1,100 yards of 'Marine Crescent' along the North Shore, with a 'High Street' to its rear, of 25 yards width and running the whole length. This latter is of course readily identified as our present day Mostyn Street. Another plan showing plots available along 'Church Street' enables the identification of some of present day Church Walks. Correlation of other streets in the particulars with our present day street layout presents difficulties, and the plan of a proposed 'Conway Street', stated to run from shore to shore and showing a line of no fewer than 31 small terraced properties along part of its length has no semblance to it at all, and we may conclude that it was soon replaced in the new plans which were drawn up in the early 1850's.

69 Brochures relating to the auction sale, held in the Llandudno Estate Office.

LLANDUDNO AND GREAT ORME'S HEAD.

MR. LLOYD

Desires respectfully to inform the Nobility, Gentry, and others, that he has been honoured with instructions to

Sell by Public Auction,

ON TUESDAY THE 28TH, AND WEDNESDAY THE 29TH AUGUST, 1849,

AT ONE O'CLOCK PUNCTUALLY EACH DAY,

AT THE CASTLE HOTEL, CONWAY,

SITES OF VALUABLE

LEASEHOLD BUILDING LAND,

IN 176 LOTS,

AT LLANDUDNO,

ON THE ESTATE OF GLODDAETH, BELONGING TO THE HONOURABLE E. M. L. MOSTYN, M.P.

SUITABLE FOR

MANSIONS, FAMILY DWELLINGS, VILLAS, AND OTHER RESIDENCES.

THE VALE OF LLANDUDNO

Is pleasantly situated in a beautiful and Romantic part of North Wales, at the foot of the Great Orme's Head. Its Shores are skirted by

LLANDUDNO AND CONWAY BAYS,

And being sheltered from the cold Northerly and Westerly Winds, the Atmosphere is at all times of the year Genial and Delightful, and it may well be called the Italy of Wales. Those stupendous triumphs of Science,

THE CONWAY SUSPENSION AND TUBULAR BRIDGES

Are in the immediate neighbourhood, and within an hour and a half's sail stand those still more magnificent Works,

THE MENAI SUSPENSION AND BRITANNIA TUBULAR BRIDGES.

The rich, wild, and majestic Mountain Scenery, the extensive Views of Land and Water, the varied Prospects, the far-famed Ruins and Antiquities, the numberless pleasant excursions, the Residences of the ancient Princes, and the salubrity and fertility of the district, are sure to draw together the Lovers of Nature, whether in the pursuit of Health, Recreation, or Retirement. Already are demands made for accommodation which cannot be provided, and, ere long, it will become the most popular Summer Resort in Wales. As a

FASHIONABLE WATERING PLACE,

It affords facilities and attractions superior to any which the Principality can boast. The Bays are peculiarly and favourably situated, so that in either, delightful

SEA BATHING

Can be enjoyed, without the slightest risk, however rough the water may be outside, as it possesses the advantage over all others of a sufficiency of water at ebb tides, and that of the most pellucid character. The thickly-wooded

GROUNDS OF GLODDAETH AND BODSCALLAN

Are in the immediate vicinity, and the noble Mansions form picturesque objects on the rising ground. The Sportsman, either in

BOATING OR FISHING,

Will find ample amusement. The present Proprietor has, at considerable expense, thoroughly drained and carefully laid out the Land which it is now proposed to sell. A splendid

MARINE CRESCENT,

With a Lawn in front, 75 feet in width, will skirt the whole of the Eastern Bay; the other Plots, with Gardens at the front and rear, running in right angles towards the Western Bay. A series of

BUILDING REGULATIONS

Have been fixed on, for the purpose of preserving the comfort of those who settle in the district, and ensuring proper ventilation, sewerage, drainage, and propriety of Fronting and Elevation, so that none shall suffer hereafter by the caprice or cupidity of others.

POWERFUL AND SWIFT STEAM-VESSELS

Land and embark Passengers Daily in Summer, and Four times a Week in Winter, to and from Liverpool; and a Landing Stage is about to be erected for the greater convenience of the Public. Llandudno is only three hours' sail from Liverpool. The

CHESTER AND HOLYHEAD RAILWAY

Is four miles distant from the town, and, by this means, direct daily communication may be had with London, Dublin, Liverpool, and all the principal Towns and Cities in the Kingdom.

Plans of the Building Sites, a Map of the Neighbourhood, the Building Regulations, with full particulars of this interesting locality, may be had on application to Messrs. WILLIAMS and M'LEOD, Solicitors, 3, Paper-buildings, London; Messrs. CUDDON, Norwich, and 8, Gray's Inn-square, London; Mr. JOHN WILLIAMS, Bodafon, Llandudno, near Conway; Messrs. WILLIAMS and JONES, Estate and Land Agents, 28, St. James's-road, Liverpool; at the principal Hotels and Newspaper-offices; or to Mr. LLOYD, Auctioneer, Park-place, Ruthin.

SMITH, ROGERSON, AND CO., PRINTERS, LORD STREET, LIVERPOOL.

Figure 11

Though it was of short lived significance, the document has considerable interest in showing some of what happened and some of what might have been. There are line illustrations of a proposed villa residence,[70] a proposed terrace and a proposed hotel, the last named to be located approximately on the site of what is now Prince Edward Square. The terrace illustration is itself anomalous in that it can in no way be related to any of the block markings of housing which are shown on the four associated plans. The illustrations are thus better described as suggestions which would be in conformity with the prescribed building regulations (see figures 12, 13 & 14).

Figure 12
Proposed Villa Residences

Figure 13
Proposed Terrace

Figure 14
Proposed Hotel

In all, the 176 lots on offer were of the massive total of 129,339 square yards, or nearly 27 acres .The land was offered leasehold for 75 years but this was "renewable upon terms similar in principle to those in daily practice by the Corporations of London, Liverpool, etc. and also by the Marquis of Westminster, Earls Derby and Sefton, and other extensive Landed Proprietors" (see figure 15). It appears that Owen Williams, at the time of the auction, was pressed to consent to alter

70 In a letter to John Williams dated 30th.October 1849, Owen Williams refers the cost of building a villa for a Mrs.Searle as being £300.

LLANDUDNO AND GREAT ORME'S HEAD,

1849.

TENURE AND BUILDING REGULATIONS FOR THE PROJECTED NEW TOWN.

The Tenure is Leasehold for 75 years, renewable upon terms similar in principle to those in daily practice by the Corporations of London, Liverpool, &c., and also by the Marquis of Westminster, Earls Derby and Sefton, and other extensive Landed Proprietors.

TABLE SHOWING THE FINE TO BE PAID FOR RENEWING A LEASE FOR SEVENTY-FIVE YEARS, WHEN PART OF THE TERM IS EXPIRED.

EXPLANATION.

To renew after 10 years have expired, look for figure 10, in the first column, and opposite this is the fraction ¼. If the rent be £10, divide the sum by 4. Thus.—

	£	s.	D.	
4)	10	0	0	Rent.
Amt. required for renewal	£2	10	0	

Again,—

To renew after 20 years have expired, look for figure 20, in the third column, and opposite this is the fraction ¾. If the rent be £40, divide the sum by ¾. Thus:—

	£	s.	D.	
¾)	40	0	0	Rent.
Amt. required for renewal	£30	0	0	

And, again,—

To renew after 63 years have expired, look for figure 63, in the seventh column, and opposite this is 9¼, which means 9¼ year's rent. If the rent be £20, multiply the same by 9¼. Thus:—

Rent per annum, £20 × 9¼ = £190.

Years Expired	Years Purchase. Common Fractions.	Years Expired	Years Purchase. Common Fractions.	Years Expired	Years Purchase. Common Fractions.	Years Expired	Years Purchase. Common Fractions.
1	1/20	20	¾	39	2 7/8	58	7 7/8
2	1/14	21	[illegible]	40	2 4/5	59	8 1/20
3	1/14	22	[illegible]	41	3 1/16	60	8¼
4	1/9	23	[illegible]	42	3¼	61	8¾
5	1/8	24	1 1/24	43	3½	62	9 1/6
6	[illegible]	25	1⅛	44	3¾	63	9¼
7	[illegible]	26	1⅕	45	3 4/5	64	9 3/5
8	[illegible]	27	1 3/11	46	4	65	10¼
9	[illegible]	28	1⅓	47	[illegible]	66	10¾
10	¼	29	1 9/20	48	[illegible]	67	11 1/11
11	[illegible]	30	1½	49	[illegible]	68	11¼
12	[illegible]	31	[illegible]	50	[illegible]	69	[illegible]
13	[illegible]	32	[illegible]	51	[illegible]	70	[illegible]
14	[illegible]	33	[illegible]	52	[illegible]	71	[illegible]
15	[illegible]	34	[illegible]	53	[illegible]	72	[illegible]
16	[illegible]	35	2¼	54	[illegible]	73	[illegible]
17	[illegible]	36	[illegible]	55	[illegible]	74	[illegible]
18	[illegible]	37	[illegible]	56	[illegible]	75	16
19	[illegible]	38	2¾	57	7½		

With a view to provide for the health and comfort of all who may visit or settle in this district, great care has been taken to provide salutary restrictions, without making them expensively irksome, and to classify the locality, assigning one neighbourhood for large houses and another for a smaller description; thereby giving protection and security to the former, without depreciating the value of the latter.

To ensure proper ventilation, the streets will be wide, and properly levelled, paved, kerbed, and the footpath flagged.

The following code of Building Regulations have been prepared and designed to ensure proper ventilation, sewerage, drainage, and uniformity of frontage and elevation, which bestow value upon property to the injury of none. In these days of sanatory reform, no doubt visitors give a preference to those watering places that are laid out on the best principles—that have wide streets and roomy and well-drained houses. It is wished that Llandudno will obtain a character as such. At the same time, on examination, the clauses will be found only reasonable, and it is to be hoped unobjectionable to any, because they have been framed with a desire that they should not have even the semblance of being arbitrary.

BUILDING REGULATIONS.

Levels of Streets.—That the levels of every new street shall be fixed by the vendor, or his surveyor for the time being; and every person who shall intend to make any new street, whether as a public way or not, shall give notice of such intention fourteen days before the commencement of such work; and every such person shall leave with the vendor a plan, drawn to a scale of not less than one inch to every ten feet, and the levels so fixed shall thereafter be kept.

New Streets.—No new street shall be made without the consent of the vendor in writing: that being obtained, it shall not be lawful to form, lay out, or build to any new street, unless the same, being a carriage road, shall be, at least, thirty-six feet wide, and have a clear space for the bed of the street, of not less than twenty-four feet in width, with a sufficient footway on each side thereof, of not less than six feet in width, clear of any steps or other projections; and in a like proportion for streets of greater width.

Back Streets.—That any streets being an approach to the back of any house in any other street, and in which back street there shall not be the principal or only entrance to any dwelling-house, may be of a width of not less than eighteen feet, if a carriage-way, and have a clear space of ten feet for the bed of the street, with a sufficient footway on each side thereof, of not less than four feet in width, clear of any steps or other projections.

Height of Houses.—No dwelling-house shall be built in any street which shall exceed in height the width of the street, and that the height of any house shall be taken from the level of the ground floor to the eave of the roof.

Court Houses.—No court or courts of houses will be permitted to be erected for habitation.

Cellars.—No cellar shall be let as a distinct or separate habitation.

Passages.—No passage at the back or side of any house or houses shall be formed of a less width than four feet, which shall be well and sufficiently, to the satisfaction of the vendor, flagged and channelled by the owner or owners of such house or houses.

Ashpits, &c.—No house shall be built without there being constructed, to the satisfaction of the vendor, in such situation as shall be appointed, a privy and ashpit with proper doors and coverings to the same.

Coal Vaults, &c.—That no vault, arch, or cellar, shall be made under any street without the written consent of the vendor, and that all vaults, arches, and cellars, shall be substantially made, so as not to interfere or communicate with any drains or sewers; and if any vault, arch, or cellar, shall be made without such written consent, then it shall be lawful for the vendor to cause the same to be filled up or demolished.

Size of Rooms and Height of Stories.—No house shall be built which shall not have at least one room on the ground floor containing one hundred and forty-four feet, superficial, clear of any stairs, or staircase, or any other reduction whatever, save one chimney breast and fireplace therein; or which shall have any living room therein which shall be less than eight feet in height, or any bed-room less than seven feet six inches, save in attic rooms, in which there shall be at least a clear height from the floor to the ridge tree of eight feet, such room, or rooms, to contain at least eighty superficial feet, and no part of such measurement shall be taken from any point which shall be less than three feet perpendicular from the surface of the flooring board to the under side of the spars. No room shall be considered an attic room, unless some part of such room is higher than the spring of the roof, and there shall in no case be more than one attic story. Cellars used as kitchens shall not be less than seven feet in height, and those not used for kitchens and habitation shall not be less than six feet in height.

Size of Windows.—Windows in rooms used for habitation shall be at least 5 feet 6 inches in height and 3 feet wide, clear of sash frames, or otherwise of an area of not less than 17 feet 6 inches, clear of the sash frame; those on the second, or bed-rooms, not to be less than 5 feet in height and 3 feet wide, or otherwise of an area of 15 feet, clear of the sash frame; and that the attic and cellar windows be not less than 3 feet square, or of an area of not less than 9 feet, clear of the sash frame. And every such window shall be a casement window, opening on hinges or pivots, unless the sashes thereof shall be double, and made so as to open both at the top and bottom.

Plans.—Before beginning to lay or dig out the foundation of any new house, or to rebuild any house, fourteen days' notice, in writing, shall be given to the vendor or his agent, by the person intending to build or rebuild such house; and every such person shall, at the same time, lodge duplicate plans and specification with the vendor or his agent for approval, drawn to a scale of not less than one inch for every six feet, which shall show the house and outbuildings, the intended situation of the privy and ashpit, drains, the thickness of the walls, the strength of timbers, the height of stories, elevations, and an area of at least one foot wide and six inches below the bottom floor round the outside of the building, except round the yard wall, which area may be covered over with flags if preferred, care being taken that the entire space be left open under the flags, and that a grating one foot square be fixed in the flagging over every such cavity, so as to admit air. No house to be built within fifteen feet, at least, of the line of street, without special permission in writing, or without a flower knot in front. That the person so lodging the plans and specification shall not consider them approved of until signed by the vendor, or his agent, when one copy will be returned and the other retained. If such building be begun of, or made without such written consent, the vendor may cause such building or drains to be demolished.

There are many advantages to the builder here over other places, inasmuch as there is abundance of stone, sand, and lime (stone) to be had on the spot. Timber is as cheap as in Liverpool, and slates are much lower in price. As in most country places, the price of labour is low as compared with that paid in large towns.

SMITH, ROGERSON, AND CO., PRINTERS, MERCURY-OFFICE, LIVERPOOL.

Figure 15

the conditions of sale so as to sell the freehold instead of the leasehold. He most emphatically refused to do so, and, many years later, stated that this was because of his opinion that the value of the property to the estate was to be in the future, for little more could have been obtained for the freehold than for the leasehold.[71]

The auction sale, which took place at Plas Mawr[72] and not at the Castle Hotel as had been advertised, appears to have aroused much interest though it resulted in only a few sales. A search for leasehold agreements which can be directly related to the auction sale has had some limited success[73] and reveals the fact that bidding must have been on a 'per square yard' basis for each lot, resulting in, for example, a purchase price of £23-16s for a 408 square yard lot, i.e. exactly 1s-2d (almost 6p) per square yard. Other examples of agreements which have been found include £133-17s-6d for 1,785 square yards (1s-6d per square yard) and £16-15s for 335 square yards (1s-0d per square yard). The locations for these three examples were on the proposed High Street (i.e. Mostyn Street), on Church Street (Church Walks) and on the Ty Draw farm near West Shore. The start of the building of modern Llandudno was thus somewhat faltering and slow, but the die was now cast and amazingly swift development was to follow during the mid and late 1850's.

There have been many attempts to pass critical judgement on the processes of enclosure, both in general terms and in the particular case of Llandudno. It is of course a fact that wastes and commons were taken and consolidated into private ownership of the big landowners. It is also doubtless true that such a process could not take place today. However, in the author's view it is futile to attempt to apply the social and other judgements of the end of the twentieth century to the situation of 150 years ago. The process of enclosure was sanctioned by the law of the land and the Mostyns as the local landowners were entitled to take advantage of this fact for whatever intended purpose. What is of more relevance is to attempt an assessment of how the result has turned out for Llandudno, and to do this one needs to consider the situation which could have developed without the enclosures.

In the 1840's there was an increasing awareness of the attractions of Llandudno, though much of the lower land was sandhills and undrained marsh. With hindsight it can be argued that eventual development was inevitable and it is surely relevant to consider how chaotic this could have been if there were no single influence having the ability to control the essential layout of the developing town and the nature of its buildings. The Mostyn presence was this influence and in the early years it was exerted both through the Estate's Agent and Architect and also personally through the Chairmanship of the Improvement Commissioners, who first met in August 1854. It can only be concluded that the generally pleasing aspect of the town is evidence in the Mostyns' favour.

Turning now to the manner in which the early town development was carried out, we may consider those who, in the words of R.Parry ('Gwalchmai') had "trespassed upon the land, on the margin of the eastern bay, and built huts and cottages, now being removed"[74].

71 'Llandudno News Sheet' of 9th.August 1882. Article by Owen Williams.

72 Plas Mawr in Conwy was built by the Wynnes of Gwydir some time prior to 1588. It became a Mostyn property after the marriage of Sir Roger Mostyn to Margaret, the Wynne heiress of Bodysgallen.

73 Documents in the Llandudno Estate Office.

An examination of the census return for 1851 shows 14 dwellings (with 18 families) listed as located on 'Morfa'. They were occupied mainly by miners and their families, and had doubtless been built under the custom of Hafod y nos,[75] already described. When the 1861 census return is examined many of these same families are to be found residing in newly built Madoc Street,[76] and an exact correlation with those in Nos.5, 12, 13, 14, 15a, 16 and 17 Madoc Street can be made. In addition there seems little doubt that the residents of 5, 19 and 20 Madoc Street are amongst those identified by Thomas Rowlands as living near the sand dunes and the sea in earlier times. There is thus conclusive proof that the displacement of families from the Llandudno Morfa was followed by rehousing in the substantial houses which we can still see today.

As further evidence in this assessment of the Llandudno enclosure it may be noted that there seems to be no record of violence or resentment associated with the development of the town. The local Mostyn Agent, John Williams, who would have been involved in all land dealings, is remembered with pleasure by Thomas Rowlands as one "willing to act as Chairman of any meeting, concert, penny reading or meeting of the Bible Society". There is also the incontrovertible fact that the local residents were among those who purchased leases and were happy to play their part in the development of Llandudno.

---

74 Taken from Llandudno: Its History and Natural History, a Llandudno Visitors' Handbook first published in 1855 by Thomas Williams of Llandudno and written by 'Gwalchmai' (R.Parry).

75 Also found written as Hafod unos, ty unnos and ty un nos.

76 Madoc Street is built on what was once a field of Pwllygwichiad Farm.

The initial slow response to the offer of plots for sale and the consequent faltering start to Llandudno's development in the early 1850's seem to have caused some indecision on the part of the Mostyns and their advisers. This is revealed in the revival of the idea of Llandudno as a commercial harbour (see figure 16).

This suggestion had been first made in 1836, when a proposal under the name of the St.George's Harbour and Railway Company suggested Llandudno as the best site for the line of communication and transport to Ireland. This was a matter which was receiving much parliamentary attention at the time and for which there were three main possibilities, these being Llandudno, Pontdinllain near to Nevin, and Holyhead. It was the last named with its shorter sea crossing that was eventually selected, even though this necessitated the bridging of both the Conway river and the Menai Straits.

The St. George's Harbour Act[77] of 20th.August 1853, though much later than the decision which had been made in favour of Holyhead as the main port for Ireland, continued with the proposal for Llandudno as a commercial port. The Company concerned was to be capitalised at £150,000, made up of 7,500 shares of £20 each, the share price being payable by instalments of £2, called for as the work proceeded. There were initially to be five directors, one of these being the Hon.Edward Mostyn Lloyd Mostyn.

ANNO DECIMO SEXTO & DECIMO SEPTIMO

VICTORIÆ REGINÆ.

Cap. ccxiii.

An Act for the Construction and Maintenance of a Harbour at *Llandudno* in the County of *Carnarvon.* [20th *August* 1853.]

WHEREAS the making of a Harbour at *Llandudno Bay* in the County of *Carnarvon* between the Points of Land known respectively as *Great* and *Little Ormes Head,* with a Branch Line of Railway or Communication to the Line of the *Chester and Holyhead* Railway, would be of great public Advantage: And whereas the Persons herein-after named, with others, are willing, at their own Cost, to carry such Undertaking into execution; but the same cannot be effected without the Authority of Parliament: May it therefore please Your Majesty that it may be enacted; and be it enacted by the Queen's most Excellent Majesty, by and with the Advice and Consent of the Lords Spiritual and Temporal, and Commons, in this present Parliament assembled, and by the Authority of the same, as follows; that is to say,

I. The several Acts of Parliament following, (that is to say,) "The Companies Clauses Consolidation Act, 1845," "The Lands Clauses Consolidation Act, 1845," "The Railway Clauses Consolidation Act, 1845," and "The Harbours, Docks, and Piers Clauses Act, 1847," shall be incorporated with and form Part of this Act. 8 & 9 Vict. cc. 16. 18. and 20., and 10 & 11 Vict. c. 27. incorporated with this Act.

[*Local.*] 43 *E* II. In

Figure 16

77 An Act for the Construction and Maintenance of a Harbour at Llandudno, in the County of Carnarvon. 16 &17 VICTORIAE Cap.ccxiii

The proposals envisaged in the Act were very comprehensive. They included any necessary 'Breakwaters, Piers, Jetties, Lighthouses and other works for safe and convenient passage of ships and other vessels into and out of the port'. There were to be 'Walls, Docks, Slips, Locks, Reservoirs, Quays, Wharfs, Moorings, Staiths, Drops, Landing Places and other Buildings and Works together with a communication by Railway to the Port and its Works'. The printed Act includes nine pages of the proposed rates for goods, ranging from Alabaster through to Zinc, and makes interesting reading as a catalogue of all conceivable items of trade for the period. If the proposals relating to the Harbour had been in any way achieved then Llandudno's Bay would have little resemblance to that which we can see today.

It is, of course, the existence of the St.George's Harbour scheme which gave rise to the well known print of what might have been in the Parade area of the town. This was to the design of Messrs.Wehnert and Ashdown and shows a railway cutting passing through what is now Prince Edward Square and approaching the Pier Entrance (see figure 17). However, it seems evident that the Harbour Scheme was even then viewed as a somewhat speculative and uncertain venture, for the Act provided that the Railway shall 'not be extended northward beyond a point nearer than one hundred yards from the back of Mostyn Street as near as may be facing Clonmel street until the Company had expended £15,000 on the Breakwaters and Roads without the consent in writing of the Hon.Edward Mostyn Lloyd Mostyn'. The approximate position of Llandudno's

Figure 17
Llandudno
After the design of Messrs.Wehnert and Ashdown.
Published by Catherall & Prichard,Chester.

eventual railway station was thus already defined in the 1853 Act.

A further provision of The St.George's Harbour Act related to the period of completion of the work envisaged. All powers granted to the Company concerning the making of the Harbour were to expire after seven years, and those relating to the making of the Railway after five years. Whilst the Company did manage to secure the Railway Branch line from Conway to Llandudno within the time, with the first Llandudno station in 1858,[78] the Harbour project was by then little advanced. The makeshift pier which was also constructed in 1858 was short-lived, being destroyed in the violent storm of 1859. (Even its actual location had been the subject of controversy, for an alternative siting opposite Clonmel Street had been suggested by the Company in 1856. This was, however, rejected by the Commissioners who insisted on the retention of the originally proposed site, beyond the Baths.) After that, the St.George's Harbour and Railway Company was at an end, for it had run out of time.

Whilst the very existence of the 1853 St.George's Harbour Act must be regarded as indicating some lingering doubts of the way in which Llandudno was to develope, the consequences of the Parliamentary Act of the next year were soon to settle the question of whether the town would be solely a watering place, or a mixed development including port facilities. This later act arose from the realisation that the transition from village to town was already taking place, and that there was a lack of any effective system of local government.

A parish meeting, described as being under the presidency of the Hon.Edward Mostyn Lloyd Mostyn was held on 6th.October 1853 and this was followed by the application to Parliament for a local Improvement Act[79] (see figure 18).

The Llandudno Improvement Act[80] was dated 3rd.July 1854, just three months after the death of the 1st.Lord Mostyn, at the age of 86. He was succeeded as 2nd.Baron by his eldest son, the Hon.Edward Mostyn Lloyd Mostyn, who up to this time had been the prime mover in the changes and developments taking place in Llandudno. As the 2nd.Baron he of course relinquished his position as a Flintshire Member of Parliament and he took up residence at the family seat of Mostyn Hall. In turn, his own son the Hon.Thomas Edward Mostyn Lloyd Mostyn took his place, both as Member of Parliament and also for the close association with Llandudno.

The stated purposes of the Llandudno Improvement Act were many in number, covering all aspects considered necessary for an orderly development of the growing town. In order to bring this about, a Board of twenty one Commissioners was to be appointed. There was to be a three year tenure of office with the annual election of seven Commissioners on the third Thursday in July.

The first Commissioners, who were all named in the actual Act, included the Hon.Thomas Edward Mostyn Lloyd Mo-

78 It is recorded that in winter, due to lack of traffic, the coaches from Llandudno Junction to Llandudno were sometimes drawn by horses. J.Roberts, Llandudno Advertiser article of 12th.March 1910.

79 The meeting is described in 'Hicklin's Illustrated Handbook of Llandudno', 2nd.Edn.1858.

80 An Act for paving, lighting, watching, draining, supplying with Water, watering, cleansing, regulating, and otherwise improving the Town of Llandudno in the County of Carnarvon, for making a cemetery, and for establishing and regulating a Market and Market Places therein; and for other Purposes. 17 & 18 VICTORIAE Cap cii.

ANNO DECIMO SEPTIMO & DECIMO OCTAVO

VICTORIÆ REGINÆ.

****

Cap. cii.

An Act for paving, lighting, watching, draining, supplying with Water, watering, cleansing, regulating, and otherwise improving the Town of *Llandudno* in the County of *Carnarvon*, for making a Cemetery, and for establishing and regulating a Market and Market Places therein; and for other Purposes. [3d *July* 1854.]

WHEREAS the Town of *Llandudno* in the Parishes of *Llandudno* and *Eglwys Rhos* in the County of *Carnarvon* contains a numerous and increasing Population, and is greatly resorted to by Persons as a Bathing and Watering Place: And whereas it would be of material Benefit and Advantage to the Inhabitants of the said Town and the immediate Vicinity thereof that certain Persons should be appointed as herein-after mentioned, with sufficient Powers, for paving, lighting, watching, draining, watering, cleansing, supplying with Water, providing a Cemetery, and for otherwise improving and regulating the same, and also for establishing, holding, and regulating a Market or Markets therein: And whereas

[*Local.*] 18 *E* Her

Figure 18

styn and also Standish Motte, Esquire, a Director of the St.George's Harbour Company. The remaining nineteen places were filled by local residents including the incumbent and perpetual curate of the parish the Rev. Edward Thomas, five esquires[81], and thirteen others bearing the title of Mr.These were all prominent citizens of the local area and so the development of the town was thus nominally in the hands of its residents. However, as will be later described, their actions were to be inextricably connected with the Mostyns, their Agents, Advisers and Trustees.

81 Esquire denoting a property holding of some acres.

The Commissioners met on 17th.August 1854, with 16 members present at this first meeting. Their first action was to elect a Chairman for the meeting (the Rev.E.T.Evans) and their second was to unanimously elect the Hon.T.E.M.Lloyd Mostyn M.P. (then aged 23½) as the Chairman of the Board. He was not then present, but is recorded in the minutes[82] as present at later meetings that year, both in September and October.

The pattern of meetings of the Commissioners was soon established, with a monthly meeting held on the last Monday of the month. Due to unfinished business, these were often adjourned, sometimes several times. In addition, there could be special meetings which were called to take specific decisions, and there was the Annual General Meeting in July with the election to replace retiring members. The electors were adult male ratepayers and also companies, whose due rates had been paid at least seven days before the election date.

It is very evident that the demands on a conscientious Commissioner's time were considerable, as the records show no fewer than 265 meetings in the seven years to July 1861. Disqualification as a Commissioner was automatic if no attendance had been made over a period of six months, and this was the fate suffered by a number of Commissioners over this period of seven years.

It is of interest to consider the status and attendance of the Hon.T.E.M.Lloyd Mostyn M.P. The minutes record that he was Chairman of the Commissioners for three periods totalling nearly six years. These were from April 1854 to July 1856, April 1857 to April 1858, and July 1858 until his untimely death in May 1861. His actual attendances at meetings of the Commissioners were few, totalling five in number, made in the years 1854, 1857 and 1858. He was in fact disqualified for non-attendance on five occasions, after three of which he was immediately re-instated to the vacancy thus created! The other two re-elections were after only short intervals so that there were only two periods totalling twelve months when he was not a Commissioner. It would, however, be totally in error to infer from this poor record of attendance that there was a lack of interest in the affairs of Llandudno on the part of the Mostyns.

The young Hon.Thomas Mostyn had married Lady Henrietta Augusta Nevill, daughter of the Earl of Abergavenny, in 1855. Whilst resident at Gloddaeth, his duties as a Member of Parliament necessitated much absence from the Llandudno area. There is, however, no doubt of his participation in matters relating to the well-being of the town, together with his wife, Lady Augusta. In addition, and of the greatest importance, there was his knowledge of the Commissioner's work, which would be passed on to him by the local Mostyn Agent and by the Mostyn Trustees and others who were invited to attend the Commissioners' meetings on many occasions.

Several references have already been made to John Williams of Bodafon, local agent for the Mostyn family. He was by now long established in the post, apparently with the full power to act on the Mostyn behalf in the sale of the numerous leases being granted at this time. His appointment as Clerk to the Board of Commissioners – a paid position at £70 per annum –

82 The minutes of the Llandudno Board of Improvement Commissioners are held in the County Record Office at Caernarfon.

was made at the very first meeting. The necessary close liaison between the Board and the Mostyn interests was thus assured. His association with the Improvement Act had, however, started earlier for the minutes of 17th.August 1854 record the payment of his expenses incurred for five journeys to London, in connection with the passage of the Act.

Examination of the Commissioners' meetings over these early years reveals an often uncomfortable state of financial affairs. The total expenses incurred in connection with the passage of the Improvement Act had been considerable and were reported at the August 1854 meeting as £1,083-10-10. These would eventually require payment, even though this seems not to have had urgency, no doubt because of the Mostyn involvement. Some small items of expenditure are detailed in the early minutes, as is the appointment of Williams Bankers of Bangor as Treasurers to the Commissioners.

The powers of the Board of Commissioners included those of raising both an Improvement Rate and a Highways Rate but these were not immediately used. Instead there were protracted investigations aimed at securing a capital loan against the security of the power to levy the Improvement Rate. The Commissioners declined to give the personal security guarantees required by the Companies first approached, and it was not until November 1856 that a draft mortgage deed for the sum of £7,000 was approved. It was later still, in March 1857, before the Commissioners' Bankers confirmed that the loan had in fact been received.

The loan was from the Law Fire Office Company and had been negotiated by Mr.Westmacott, a London Solicitor and a Trustee and Adviser to the Mostyns. Until Mr.Westmacott's death in 1860 there was to be much correspondence with him, on many subjects. On the matter of the loan, he was first asked to negotiate for this in October 1855, and from March 1856 the references indicate the increasing urgency of the matter. Whilst the records do not show great speed of action on Mr.Westmacott's part, it must be noted that the Commissioners themselves had decided that they would not pay an interest rate above 5%.

It was in June 1856 that the Commissioners called upon their Clerk, John Williams, to identify the extent of their first two years of expenditure, and to estimate the needs for the coming year of 1856-57. By this time the sum of £1,964-17-10 (including the cost of the Act itself and the commencement costs for the sewerage scheme) could be identified as already expended and chargeable against the capital loan. The sum of £236-1-8 chargeable to the Improvement Rate had also been used, whilst £143-3-6 was already chargeable to the Highways Rate. John Williams' forecasts for the 1856-57 year were for an Improvement need of £771-8-8 (and hence a total requirement of £1,007-10-4) and a Highways need of £138 (which gave a total requirement of £281-3-6). It may be noted that his Improvement Rate calculations included £350 for interest at 5% on the pending capital loan, and a contribution to a sinking fund for the loan's repayment over thirty years (i.e. £233-6-8, this being one-thirtieth of £7,000)

The Commissioners accepted completely the figures provided by their Clerk and decided on a single combined rate of 2s-6d in the £1, as being necessary to cover the total requirement of £1,288-13-10. It may thus be concluded that the total rateable value for the residential properties in Llandudno was of the order of £10,000 in 1856. This first rate was to be payable in three equal instalments, due on 1st.July, 1st.November and 1st.March. It was, however, to prove to be no easy task to extract the rates at their due times from the Llandudno ratepayers.

At the same time, i.e. late in 1856, as the final arrangements for the £7,000 loan were being made, the major capital project of the Sewerage Scheme was agreed, with an accepted tender price of £7,600. The inevitable shortfall in the capital that would be needed to pay for this does not appear to have been considered until a year later.

However, in November 1857, Mr.Westmacott was asked to arrange a further loan of £3,000 at the same rate and a second mortgage deed to the Law Fire Office, again requiring repayment over 30 years, was eventually sealed on 31st.May 1858. By this time, as will be related, there had already been major problems of payment for the work done, with threats of litigation.

With the exeption of the year 1857 when the estimates were delayed until the Autumn, it became the practice for them to be made soon after the July elections and the consequent nomination of members of the Finance Committee. By the year 1861, after a 10% increase due to the previous year's new valuations, the total rateable value for Llandudno was recorded as being £14,480. This increase was of course in keeping with the rapid growth of the town.

In June 1856 a Collector of Rates was first appointed. There was only one applicant, a David Williams. Though there is reference to an apparent dilatoriness in paying money into the bank in May 1858, he was to remain in the post for a number of years. His appointment was initially at a salary of £20 per annum plus the small commission of 5 shillings per £100 collected and he was moved to complain of this small remuneration in January 1860. The Commissioners responded by increasing his commission to £2-10-0 % on the rates collected. This was then a handsome reward, albeit for a difficult and unpopular job. There are regular references in the minutes to the Collector's reports on unpaid rates, and in each year from 1857 there are minutes concerning the threats of summonses, or instructions as to the actual taking out of them. The money outstanding near the end of the rating year is reported as £700 in 1860 but there was an improved situation in 1861 when the figure was only £242.

It seems fair to comment that the financial affairs of the Board of Commissioners proceeded on a 'hand to mouth' basis in these early years. The receipt of the initial loan of £7,000 enabled payment of the Parliamentary Agents in early 1857, together with stage payments for the sewerage scheme amounting to some £5,700 by Autumn 1857. However, in October 1857 the Clerk John Williams was mandated to call on Williams Bankers to arrange further advances until the second loan became available. At best, he can have had only limited success for by January 1858, with the main sewerage scheme now completed, the Contractor's own Solicitors were demanding the final payment. At this same time, the Clerk was instructed to respond to the various letters demanding payments due, with a reference to their 'early attention'. The drastic step of the temporary suspension of 'all present works and outlays' was also taken.

The recorded details of the lengthy negotiations – from November 1857 to May 1858 – for the second loan make surprising reading. In February 1858 the Clerk wrote to Mr.Westmacott that the Commissioners relied on him to get the loan and so avoid litigation. Further letters followed in March and April and in a desperate action a letter of application was sent by the Commissioners on 14th.April directly to the Law Fire Office. The result was a letter from Mr.Westmacott stating that if the Commissioners wanted the loan they must desist from such direct communication to the Law Fire Office, as it would only impede. He had therefore instructed the Secretary at the Office to withhold it!

The further loan of £3,000 was eventually made, after provision of the various declarations concerning the Rateable Property of the town by the Clerk and the Valuation Committee. Even so, the financial problems were not yet over, because of the slow payment of the rates. In August 1858 it proved necessary to obtain a £300 loan from the Williams Bank, against the security of a bond signed by all Commissioners. One signatory was the Hon.Thomas Mostyn who had attended and chaired the Commissioners' meeting at which this was authorised. The bond for this short term loan was redeemed in December 1858, as the financial position improved with the collection of the rates.

It seems clear that from 1859 onwards there was an increasing confidence in financial matters on the part of the Commissioners, for at a special meeting held on 30th.September 1859 the one subject was the advisability of applying for Parliamentary authority to borrow the very large sum of £25,000. The discussion paper presented by a Commissioner envisaged the use of the money for the purchase of the Water Works and Gas Works, together with the Market Hall. The last named would also be enlarged and a Town Hall and Slaughter Houses would be built. The calculations presented purported to show that the resulting income would adequately service the cost of the loan. The view of Mr.Westmacott was that such an appeal to Parliament would be advantageous, and, indeed, necessary, sooner or later. However, caution prevailed, and the subject was deferred.

At this time there had been no reference to the existence of any actual sinking fund, other than the fact that it was two years in arrears by August 1859. There had thus been no lessening of the capital debt of £10,000, though of course half yearly interest on the two sums borrowed had been regularly paid. This was naturally a cause for concern and in September 1860 it was recorded that the Law Fire Office was agreeable to repayments of sums of one-thirtieth of the combined loans, at the Commissioners' convenience. The first such repayment of £333-6-8 was made in October 1860, with further similar repayments in December 1860 and November 1861. Thus by the end of 1861 Llandudno's indebtedness had been reduced to £9,000, this being effected by the Commissioners' caution and the avoidance of further capital borrowing.

It has already been stated that the first plans for Llandudno's development were those prepared by Owen Williams, a member of the Liverpool firm of Williams and Jones. These were prepared for the 1849 land auction and, as we have seen, resulted in the sale of a number of leases over the years immediately following.

By the time of the passage of the Llandudno Improvement Act, the Mostyns had commissioned other professional assistance. A new overall plan for the town had been drawn up by the Architects and Surveyors, Messrs. Wehnert and Ashdown, of Charing Cross, London. Their well known view of Llandudno as it will be was published, and original copies in various sizes of this most interesting print are not hard to come by. Comment has already been made in a previous chapter that whilst the design showed the full range of sea front buildings, the St.George's Harbour Railway is also shown, with the line passing between the North and South Parades before entering the unshown obscurity of the area below camera hill.

Drainage and Sewerage

As a necessary consequence of the Improvement Act, the services of Mr.F.Macdougall Smith C.E. had been engaged by the Commissioners in October 1854 to prepare plans, sections and levels of Llandudno. The cost of this survey was £364-6-11 and it was complete by Spring 1855. In August 1855 he was asked to plan for drainage - and also to investigate the Gogarth Water Supply, of which more will be written later. In his contemporary handbook,[83] Hicklin describes these prepared plans as being for "domestic and sanitory purposes" and declares them to be "comprehensive and complete." The drainage scheme is described as a "reservoir main sewer with collateral drains from the Main Parade at the Orme's Bay to the Conway Bay into which they are discharged at about three quarters ebb tide."

The Commissioners were soon considering the implementation of the sewerage scheme. They were prepared to start the work in September 1855, but this was delayed because of a conflict between the sewerage plans and those of the St.George's Harbour Company.

This conflict in the plans concerned the eastern Gloddaeth Street area, where the work was to be started. In November 1855 Wehnert informed the Commissioners that Macdougall Smith had been a consenting party to "the line of the Railway along Gloddaeth to the Parade." Smith's reply was that this was "an impudent and wilful falsehood" and "an abominable statement. It was only Wehnert who had marked it on the plan in January, saying it was Lord Mostyn's wish." In Smith's view it would "ruin Llandudno as a bathing place." He believed that Wehnert was "with the interests of the Railway Company, would decline to meet him and would sue if his own professional reputation should suffer."

The Commissioners sought the advice of Mr.Westmacott whose responses indicate the indecision and debate that must have been taking place between the Company and the Mostyns. He first gave his opinion that the Commissioners could proceed with safety with the main sewer, but he referred shortly afterwards to the possibility of litigation if it were commenced without a proper understanding with the Railway Company. With the Hon.Thomas Mostyn's agreement, in December 1855 the plans to commence the sewerage scheme were in fact suspended until a

83 'Hicklin's Illustrated Handbook of Llandudno', 2nd.Edn. 1858.

satisfactory undertaking or indemnity had been obtained.

The situation was resolved in February 1856 when agreement was reached between Westmacott and Macdougall Smith with the Railway Company, that the main sewer would be as the original plan.

Soon after this time the Commissioners' relations with Macdougall Smith appear to have deteriorated, for they were slow in paying his accounts for the earlier work done. The good offices of Mr.Westmacott were sought, he being asked to explain the steps that were then being taken, through himself, to secure the £7,000 loan. In the event the necessary cheque for Smith's earlier work was eventually sent in May 1856, and it is recorded that if the Bank were not to honour it, the Rev.E.T.Evans would lend the money to the Commissioners.

For the closing months of 1856 there are numerous references in the minutes to the sewerage project. In September the negotiations with Macdougall Smith established that his terms for supervising the scheme would be 3 guineas per day, exclusive of his travelling and other expenses. However, at about the same time, it was decided that although the work was to be advertised for tenders in accordance with the Macdougall Smith specifications and plans, a work superintendent would also be appointed.

Tenders for the work were received by late October 1856 but their consideration was deferred until the question of supervision was resolved. There were 43 applications for the position of Clerk of Works, from which a J.H.Colbran of Rugby was selected. At this time the Commissioners appear to have been in two minds as to whether they might save the expense of professional supervision by an Engineer, by using a competent Clerk of Works. This was despite the known views of Macdougall Smith, who emphasized that the work required great care and supervision, and that he could not be held responsible unless he could from time to time test the efficiency. This news was evidently relayed to Mr.Westmacott, who in a letter of 3rd.November 1856, enquired whether or not it was the intention of the Commissioners to use Macdougall Smith's services. After hearing of the Commissioners' financial concerns, Mr.Westmacott was soon able to inform that Macdougall Smith was willing to superintend the main sewer work for a fee of 100 guineas. An assurance was also given that that the Mostyns would forego any charges for surface damage relating to the land under which the sewers were to be carried. These arrangements proved satisfactory to the Commissioners and, in a reversal of their earlier decision, John Williams was instructed to inform the unfortunate Colbran that his services would not now be required.

By the end of December 1856 the way forward for the long delayed scheme was finally clear. The Lord High Admiral had by then approved the foreshore plans, and, on Macdougall Smith's advice, there had been a re-advertisement seeking tenders for the work. This had resulted in eight replies, with the tenders ranging from £6,820 to £14,588-7-6. The smallest of these did not stand up to scrutiny and so that of Edwin Knight of Manchester in the sum of £7,600-3-5 was accepted. His sureties proved to be acceptable, the agreement was sealed on 11th.February 1857 and the work commenced.

Whilst Macdougall Smith was in frequent attendance, the day to day work was in the charge of a James Barnes who had been appointed on Smith's recommendation as Clerk of Works at 2 guineas per week. He was soon found to be unsatisfactory, due to intemperance, and is recorded as being dismissed by 13th.March. A Henry McCall was engaged in his place and some early unsatisfactory work was rectified. Progress was then rapid, and, as has already been recorded, the stage payments made by Autumn 1857 amounted to some £5,700.

It seems clear that the Macdougall Smith supervision was both competent and thorough. He strongly recommended to the Commissioners that private house drainage should be carried out simultaneously with the main drainage work, and for this, Mr.Knight's tender of 3s-11d per lineal yard was accepted. He found it necessary to recommend some variations and additions to the main sewer plan, which were accepted as desirable by the Commissioners. They were, however, loth to authorise any extra costs and so a replacement plan involving deletions and substitutions was approved. Unfortunately, in early September 1857 the contractor Mr.Knight declined to carry out the proposed in lieu works, and claimed compensation for profit on works suspended. This was to be the start of the major payment problems already referred to in the narrative, and which dragged on for several months.

It was not until the 28th.October 1857 that a meeting of all parties concerned with the disputed matters could be arranged. This was chaired by the Hon.Thomas Mostyn. An offer of £350 against Mr.Knight's claim of £602 was accepted but a subsequent letter from him made it clear that he would charge interest at 9% on any money withheld after becoming due. This was agreed by the Commissioners who were by now again dependent upon the efforts of Mr.Westmacott, this time to secure the second loan of £3,000.

As already detailed, the cash shortage was to remain critical through the months of the winter of 1857/58. By 25th.January 1858, Mr.Knight's solicitors, Messrs.Cobbett and Wheeler, were seeking his payments. The mediation of the Mostyn Solicitor Mr.Westmacott was again necessary and it was not until the 9th.June 1858 that the Commissioners received the final confirmation that Mr.Knight had been fully paid.

The saga of the main sewerage scheme is thus not one which reflects unqualified credit upon the Commissioners. However, the end result was praiseworthy, for in December 1857 Macdougall Smith had reported the sewerage system to be satisfactory and in good order. As will also be detailed later in the narrative under the heading of houses and roads, the necessary connections of the private houses to the system were also well under way.

Water Supply

As has already been noted, one of the specific purposes of the Improvement Act was to ensure that adequate arrangements would be made for the supply of water to the town.

At the time of enclosure it seems that the water sources for the village were adequate for the then population, with a considerable number of wells available at not too great a distance. It is of interest to consider these wells and their locations and the information given in articles[84] in the Llandudno Advertiser in 1909 is of value

84 Articles in series 'Llandudno as it was' by John Roberts in Llandudno Advertiser issues in October and November 1909.

here. The list is not exhaustive, but includes most of the better known wells.

Ffynnon-y-Cwm: This well is found near the gas works, between the works and the farm on the side of the hill. It is very ancient and is mentioned in early Welsh history, being referred to by Robin Ddu who flourished in the 13th.Century. (The same sage is also said to have predicted bridges over both the Conway river and the Menai Straits). The water was reputedly the very best for tea-making. It is said that good housewives would on special occasions send their husbands all the way to this well for water.

Ffynnon-y-Gaseg (The Mare's Well): Situated on the extreme northwestern part of the Orme, on the Marine Drive and apparently used as a horse drinking fountain at the time the articles were written. The origin of the name is not known, but it is in close proximity to prehistoric remains and so may well have been used in ancient times.

Ffynon Galchog (The Limey Well): Situated on the flat ground below Penymynydd Farm, to the North East. The water was considered very good, and was believed beneficial to children's bones and teeth. It is said to date from Roman times and was certainly used by the miners for the washing of copper ore. The well was supposedly never dry even in the greatest droughts.

Ffynnon Gwerddglod-yr-egin (The well of the Green Meadows): This was described in the article as found by "crossing by the path on the left of Conway Road, which leads to Queen's Road, on coming to the Queen's Road end and walking a few paces to the left we come to the well." Again this well was stated to have good water even when many other wells were dry.

Ffynnon Llety Madoc (The well of Madoc's Abode): Later to be known as Ffynnon Rhufeinig or the Roman Well, another of the wells on the Great Orme, this was described in 1909 as in a recess in the enclosure wall of the Great Orme Golf Course.

The remains of habitations nearby are reputedly those of the Abode of Madoc – either Madoc of Gloddaeth or his father Madoc ap Iorwerth Goch of Creuddyn, who flourished in the 13th.Century and is said to have used the Great Orme as a deer ranch.

Ffynnon Mair (Mary's Well): This is near to Llanrhos Church, which is also known as St.Mary's Church, and was no doubt used by the church in ancient times. The field nearby is called "Gardd y Mynach" (The Monk's Garden) so there may well have been an abbey nearby, which would also have used the well. (n.b. This well has recently been restored and is now an interesting feature in the walk across the corner of the field on the opposite side of the road to the Llanrhos Church).

Ffynnon-yr-Odyn (The Kiln's Well): In the 1909 article this well is stated to be in the grounds of a house in Church Walks but it is now to be found in the grounds of the new St.George's school. It seems probable that the name is due to its close proximity to numerous lime kilns that were at one time in the area. It is another well that has been the subject of recent renovation.

Ffynnon Powel (Powell's Well): This is described as found by walking along the path from Penymynydd to St.Tudno's Church, when just in sight of the church. It was stated to have been a great favourite of the old inhabitants, being palatable and sweet. It was supposedly so called because very long ago there was a nearby dwelling occupied by a small farmer and his family of the name of Powell. The legend has it that they were in dire straits in a time of drought, prayed for deliverance and on returning home found the spring bubbling up near to their door.

Ffynnon Sadwrn (Saturn's Well): This is located near to the Little Orme, in the vicinity of Brynybia, near to the present Aber Drive. The article's writer deplored the fact that even then, in l909, the well was partly closed and the spring nearly extinct due to excavation and the laying of drains in the area. He also speculated on the origin of the name, listing the possibilities of worship of Saturn as a deity, or perhaps some Roman festival.[85] The well is stated to have been much used and never dry in the older times, it being particularly valued for the brewing of beer. The well is now remembered by the existence of Ffynnon Sadwrn Lane.

Ffynnon Tudno (St.Tudno's Well): Situated a short distance to the east of St.Tudno's Church, and undoubtedly connected with it by the use of the water for religious purposes.

Ffynnon Wen (The White Well): This was situated in Old Road and supplied a fountain in the wall on the right hand side going up. The water source can be traced up the side of Pen-y-Dinas, the site of an ancient hill fort. The article suggests that the well may have provided the water supply for the fort and further speculates on possible uses for rites and worship purposes, because of the close proximity of the rocking stone.

Whilst the above list is of those described in the Llandudno Advertiser articles, there are of course other wells whose names can be found. In a publication of 1861[86] there is reference to *Ffynnon-gwain-fugail (The Meadow Shepherd's Well)* and to *Ffynnon Llygaid (The Eye Well)*, both presumably then well known and available for use. However, the well that was to become of major importance, and which was referred to by both of the quoted sources was the *Ffynnon Ogarth (The Gogarth Well, or Spring)*: This is the 'Public Spring' which was marked on Richard Yates's Enclosure Map of April 25th.1848, and which was allocated, with one perch of land, to the inhabitants of the parish as a well or watering place.

It is thus a matter of no surprise to find that the Commissioners were concerned at a very early stage to find some means whereby the Gogarth Water source could be utilised for the rapidly growing town – which was, however, at some distance away. They were also concerned with the purity of the supply and quickly submitted a sample for analysis. The results, obtained by a Mr.William Herapath of Bristol, were very satisfactory and in October 1854 the Commissioners printed 500 copies of the analysis. It is recorded that a copy was provided to each lodging house and hotel-keeper. This analysis, together with Mr.Herapath's favourable comments, was for some years to feature prominently in the descriptive literature concerning the town. The analysis showed there to be some 18.4 grains of dissolved substances per gallon with a hardness of 15 degrees, reduced to 5 degrees after boiling. the purity thus being incontestably demonstrated. Mr.Hera-

85 Whilst there have been such suggestions linking the well name to the Roman festival, a stronger case can be made for it being named after Sadwrn (ca 525 A.D.), the brother of Illtud, one of the early Welsh saints. Yet another explanation is related to the well's major usage on a Saturday, when water was drawn for the weekend.

86 Llandudno: Its History and Natural History, a Llandudno Visitors' Handbook by R. Parry. 2nd.Edn. 1861.

path is quoted as considering the Gogarth Springs equal to the celebrated Bristol water (see figure 19).

It is difficult, in our present day, to visualise the problems that were soon to be experienced concerning the water supply for the rapidly increasing population and the Summer visitors. Whilst there were no doubt a number of small private wells, many of them will have been of dubious quality and of irregular supply. The transport of water from the public sources, had, of course, long been part of the daily life in the area.

	Grains.
Chloride of Calcium	0.163
Sulphate of Magnesia	1.433
Common Salt	5.643
Organic matters	0.326
Nitrates	Traces
Carbonate of Lime	9.963
Sulphate of Lime	0.433
Oxide of Iron	0.003
Silica	0.463
	18.427

Figure 19

In May 1855 the Commissioners' Clerk was asked to obtain Mr.Westmacott's opinion concerning their powers to erect a water works. There is no record of the reply, but there is ample evidence of the increasing problems being faced by the Commissioners. Water samples from Brookes's Well, Shaft Tai Newyddion and Tyn-y-Pwll Well were sent to Mr.Herapath for analysis. (The charge was unexpectedly high at 9 guineas, which was later queried). An experimental shaft was also sunk, with Mostyn consent, at Tyn-yr-hwlfa, site of an old small farm, a little higher up Old Road than the King's Head. In September 1855, after many public complaints, a water sub-committee was formed. One of its first recommendations was for a John Hughes to be engaged to pump water from Brookes's Well, for public use. This was to be done until 1st.November, 3 hours a.m. and 3 hours p.m., at a wage of 15s a week, with an extra man to help on Saturdays, at 2s-6d.

At much the same time, as has already been earlier stated, Mr.Macdougall Smith was asked to report and plan for the use of the Gogarth spring. He was also specifically asked to find in his investigations the extent of the interest in the Gogarth Spring Water of the Old Mine, the landowner John Lloyd Jones, and, later, the Bishop of Bangor.

By March 1856 it was clear that the major interest – which would require considerable compensation – was that of the Old Mine. Their 'Tom and Jerry' device which has been mentioned in an earlier chapter, had been constructed to use the motive power of the Gogarth Spring to pump water from the flooding mine shafts.

During the ensuing summer of 1856 the necessity for further public water supply was met by the installation of a public pump "in the back street from Old Road to Llewelyn Street" (i.e. Water Street), and a further well with a pump was sunk at the back of Ty Fry at a cost of some £45. However by now it was clear to the Commissioners that their involvement in another major public undertaking, in addition to the sewerage scheme, was better avoided at this time.

On 4th.August 1856 notice was given of a motion to devolve the Commissioners' powers to a Company, or Companies, for the erection of both Water Works and Gas Works. Later in the same month the resolution was passed unanimously, and as a result the Llandudno Water and Gas Company came into being. It appears that the resolution alone enabled the establishment and operation of the Company, for it was not until the Spring of 1859 that the agreement delegating the Commissioners' powers was formally concluded.

Whilst the author has personally found no record of the way in which the Company resolved the interests in the Gogarth Supply, it seems that a sum of £750 was received in 1856 by the owners of the Old Mine.[87] It is certainly evident that the necessary work was proceeding during 1857. In September of that year the Commissioners authorised the Company to "lay down fire plugs as the work proceeds". A Macdougall Smith plan for locating 30 of these was approved, and 30 hydrants costing £3-5-0 each were authorised. The installation was carried out by Messrs Easton and Amos, who were the contractors to the Water and Gas Company. Some 300 feet of the necessary rivetted leather hose were purchased in 1859 after the completion of the work, and further hydrants were installed in 1861.

It is again convenient to have recourse to the Hicklin Handbook of Llandudno[88] for a description of the water supply at this time.

"The water supply is obtained and conveyed by gravitation, from the Gogarth Springs, near the top of the Great Orme's Head, to a storage reservoir at Tyn-y-Coed, which is about 350 feet above the level of the sea; thus giving a sufficient pressure of water to reach the highest dwelling for sanatory purposes, and also as a guarantee from danger in cases of fire. The details of these works embrace all the engineering improvements of modern science, the plan and survey having been designed and prepared by the eminent engineer before named, who has carried out similar works with decided success in various parts of the kingdom."

The Commissioners' relations with the Water and Gas Company appear to have been on an amicable and professional basis. In November 1859 one of the Commissioners' Office Rooms in Church Walks was relinquished for the Company's use. There are also several references to enquiries about the use of of any waste or surplus water for flushing purposes to the drainage system. On occasion, the Company consented to such use (at 10d per 1,000 gallons) when their supplies were satisfactory i.e. "not less than 13'6" depth in the large reservoir."

That this was not always so, is evidenced by the records during what must have been a very dry summer in 1861. In July of that year there were complaints of the water being warm and there was only one period of supply in each day. The Commissioners respectfully asked for this to be varied to two periods per day, if necessary these to be of the shorter periods of 1½ hours each. The Company cooperated for a time but was then compelled to return to supplying only once a day, as their reservoir level was so low. The situation evidently remained critical for some time and by 26th.August there is reference to the suspension of the supply to builders and to the pony stand! Still later, in November of the same year, the Commissioners agreed to the use of the public pump to supply the Company's reservoir, in the case of the Gogarth Spring being insufficient to meet the requirements of the town.

It can thus be noted that by the early 1860's great collaborative efforts were be-

87 Information given in 'The Great Orme Copper Mines' by Don Smith. Creuddyn Publications 1988.

88 'Hicklin's Illustrated Handbook of Llandudno', 2nd.Edn. 1858.

ing made to ensure an adequate water supply for the developing town. The inherent problems were, however, to remain for many years and were not adequately solved until 1880 when the lake supply which has continued to this present day was obtained.

Gas Supply

It was as early as the meeting of October 1855 that the Commissioners first received a proposal to erect a Gas Works. Consideration was then deferred and it was the next year in June 1856 when a Gas Engineer, George Walcott, submitted that this should be done by a joint stock company. The proposal was to be fully considered after the then pending July elections and was doubtless a factor in the already mentioned decision, taken in August 1856, to devolve the Commissioners' powers relating both to Water and Gas. It seems that the construction of the Gas Works proceeded with little incident and its location is described by the informative Hicklin Hand Book as "in the vicinity of the town, on the Conway Road."

In March 1859, John Williams as Clerk to the Commissioners was required to approach the Water and Gas Company for information about the possible supply of gas to light the town, and the price of each such lamp. Matters moved rapidly and by May the Commissioners had agreed to purchase 40 lamps and posts at a cost of £3-3-0 each, with equal payments over 3 years at 5% interest. In June a lamppost siting committee was formed.

The necessarily prudent financial approach of the Commissioners is typified by the actions taken in August and September 1859. John Williams was to check on gas contracts made elsewhere and he then duly reported the arrangements that had recently been made at Rhyl. There, the contract was for £100 to light 40 lamps for 9 months, with 5 nights at the full of the moon when they were not lit. A little negotiation with the Water and Gas Company resulted in agreement that the 40 lamps in Llandudno would be lit for £90 from September to 1st.June, with 7 nights not lit at the full of the moon. The lighting time was to be "as the St.Helens timetable" , with the lamps being put out at 1 a.m.

It appears that this contract was a matter of annual negotiation. In September 1860 the cost was to be £2-10-0 per lamp (and 2s-6d for two coats of paint, one in Autumn, one in Spring, the latter to be of "a good stone colour"). In 1861 the negotiations were somewhat less favourable, and the agreed price of £3 per lamp was with the additional proviso for "earlier extinguishing when moon is up, on nights after the full". Despite this, on 20th.October 1861 the Commissioners resolved to have a further 4 gas lamps in the town.

As has already been stated, the overall plan for Llandudno was that drawn up for the Mostyns by Wehnert and Ashdown, a London firm of Architects and Surveyors. The leases on the building plots were granted on terms agreed between the purchaser and John Williams, the local Mostyn Agent, who by 1854 was acting with very considerable authority on behalf of the Hon.T.E.M.Lloyd Mostyn. The price per square yard at this time does not appear to have changed from the range of 1s to 1s-6d per square yard which had been bid at the auction in 1849.

In the earlier leases the usual term was for 75 years, at a yearly rental of 5s. However, this was not invariably so, for a 60 year lease granted as late as 1851 has been noted. (The term of 60 years appears to have been that normally in use on the estate, prior to its enlargement by the enclosure award). Again, it was not long before leases of 99 years were being granted, and such agreements dating from 1855 have been found. It is also evident that leases for both 75 and 99 years were being granted at the same time, over a considerable period of years.

Whilst a number of the Commissioners were involved in early purchases of leases, those made by the Rev.E.T.Evans M.A., the incumbent of the parish, are of interest and typical of the time. He made separate purchases of adjacent plots fronting on Church Walks, as it was being developed. His first purchase was of a 75 year lease in December 1853, and the second, with Church Walks itself now being named, was of a 99 year lease in April 1855. Copy agreements relating to these purchases are reproduced (see figures 20 & 21)and it may be noted that the second document was witnessed by Frederick Wehnert, the London planner for the Mostyns. The Rev.Evans's participation in the development of Llandudno, though significant, was soon to be cut short, for he died on 21st.April 1857 whilst on a visit to Rome. At the time of his death he was in fact the Chairman of the Llandudno Board of Commissioners, and subsequently the Hon.T.E.M.Lloyd Mostyn was re-elected to replace him as both a Commissioner and Chairman.

In an earlier chapter reference has been made to the fact that the 75 year leases were renewable. The terms for renewal, together with the detail of the building regulations – which were stringent for the time – were incorporated in the Conditions of Sale provided to each purchaser. Paragraph 2 of these conditions, which has been reproduced, reveals the continuing uneasy state of affairs relating to the Mostyn mortgaged estates, in that there is need for reference to the 1793 will of Sir Roger Mostyn together with the naming of the then principal holders of mortgages relating to the Gloddaeth Estate[89] (see figures 22 & 23).

Throughout the early years of Llandudno's development there could be no more vital areas of cooperation between the Improvement Commissioners and the Mostyn Estate than those concerned with housing and the new streets of the town. From a study of the available records the author has no doubts that this necessary cooperation was fully present.

It seems probable that the first large houses to be built in the new town were those of Vine House and Haley House in Church Walks.[90] For these, as for all new

89 There are numerous contemporary documents held in the Clwyd Record Office at Hawarden which relate to the complex financial position of the various estates of the Mostyn family at this time, but they are not otherwise relevant to this narrative concerning Llandudno.

buildings the regulations were very clear in stating that the levels of every new street would be fixed by the vendor. It is also evident that the estate's responsibility for each new road or street was to prepare it to an acceptable condition when it might then be "taken to" (i.e. adopted) by the Town Commissioners. This process commenced as early as August 1855 when the Commissioners authorised a survey, by Mr.Ellis Williams of Llanrwst, of parts of the Esplanade, Mostyn Street and Church Walks. The resulting report found fault with the latter, and the Mostyn adviser Mr.West-

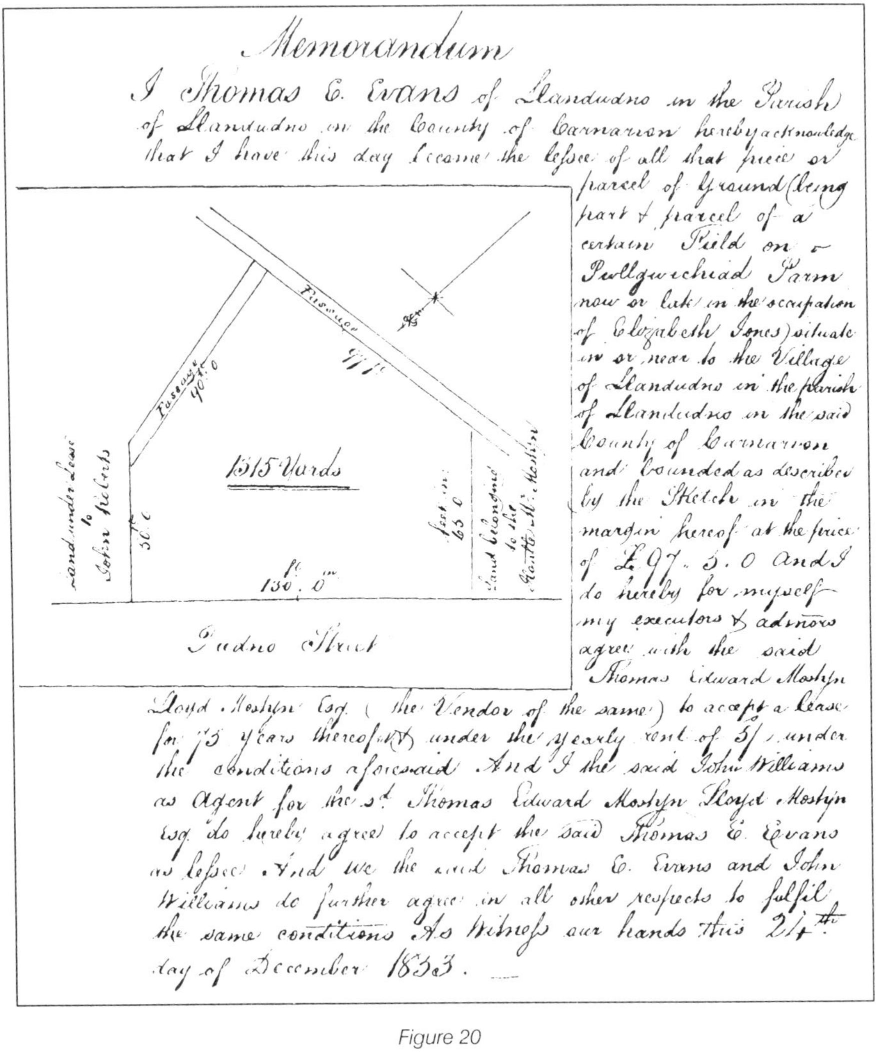

Memorandum

I Thomas E. Evans of Llandudno in the Parish of Llandudno in the County of Carnarvon hereby acknowledge that I have this day become the Lessee of all that piece or parcel of Ground (being part & parcel of a certain Field on Pellgwrchiad Farm now or late in the occupation of Elizabeth Jones) situate in or near to the Village of Llandudno in the Parish of Llandudno in the said County of Carnarvon and bounded as described by the Sketch in the margin hereof at the price of £97. 5. 0 And I do hereby for myself my executors & admors agree with the said Thomas Edward Mostyn Lloyd Mostyn Esq. (the Vendor of the same) to accept a Lease for 75 years thereof [illegible] under the yearly rent of 5/ , under the conditions aforesaid And I the said John Williams as Agent for the sd Thomas Edward Mostyn Lloyd Mostyn Esq. do hereby agree to accept the said Thomas E. Evans as Lessee And we the said Thomas E. Evans and John Williams do further agree in all other respects to fulfil the same conditions As Witness our hands this 24th day of December 1853.

Figure 20

90 Article in series 'Llandudno as it was' by John Roberts in Llandudno Advertiser issue of 15th May 1909.

macott was duly informed of the need for some remedial work. Mr.Ellis Williams was eventually appointed to the official position of Surveyor of Roads in August 1856, which he held for a period of one year at a salary of £10. From October 1857, as will be detailed later, the position of Surveyor of Roads was combined with certain other duties.

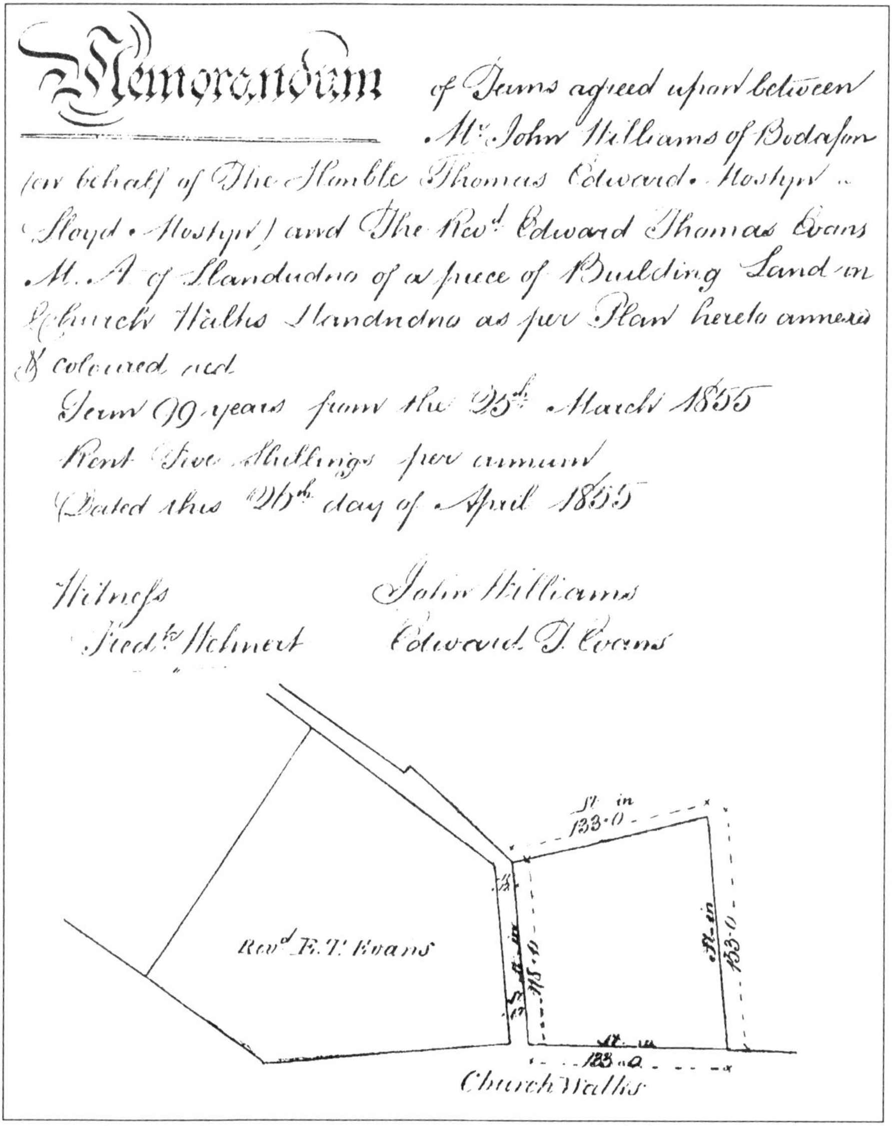

Memorandum of Terms agreed upon between Mr. John Williams of Bodafon for behalf of The Honble Thomas Edward Mostyn Lloyd Mostyn) and The Revd. Edward Thomas Evans M.A of Llandudno of a piece of Building Land in Church Walks Llandudno as per Plan hereto annexed & coloured red.

Term 99 years from the 25th March 1855

Rent Five Shillings per annum

Dated this 26th day of April 1855

Witness Fredk. Helmert

John Williams

Edward T. Evans

Figure 21

CONDITIONS OF SALE

OF

BUILDING GROUND,

The Property of Thomas Edward Mostyn Lloyd Mostyn, Esq.,

SITUATE AT LLANDUDNO IN THE SEVERAL PARISHES

OF

EGLWYS RHOS AND LLANDUDNO, IN THE COUNTY OF CAERNARVON,

FOR A RENEWABLE TERM OF 75 YEARS.

II.—The vendor will furnish to each purchaser, or his solicitor, an abstract of the title to the lot or lots sold to him. Where the purchase-money shall not exceed 300*l.*, such abstract shall only be of a deed of conveyance of the said building ground, dated the 31st day of October 1857, and made between Thos. Austen and Thos. Alcock, Esquires, of the 1st part, William Wellesley Knighton, Bart., of the 2nd part, Michael Seymour, a Capt. in her Majesty's Royal Navy, of the 3rd part, Thomas Charles Harrison, Esq., and the said Thos. Alcock, of the 4th part, the said Sir William Wellesley Knighton and Charles Parke, Esq., of the 5th part, John Squire, Esq., James Parke, Gent., and Edmund Robins, Auctioneer, of the 6th part, George Freeth, Gent., and William Parke, the younger, Gent., of the 7th part, Sir William Foster, Bart., of the 8th part, the Hon. E. M. Ll. Mostyn, of the 9th part, the above named vendor of the 10th. part, and Cynric Lloyd, Esq., of the 11th part. The vendor will furnish to each purchaser, or his solicitor, an abstract of the title to the lot or lots sold to him; but such purchaser may, at his own expense, have the like abstract of title as if he were a large purchaser. Where the purchase-money shall exceed 300*l.* the abstract shall commence with the will of Sir Roger Mostyn in 1793; but each purchaser shall assume without further proof (in order to prevent delay and expense) that Sir Roger Mostyn, at the date of his will and death, was seised in fee-simple in possession, and that all the limitations in a settlement of 1766 therein referred to had failed or determined, nor shall the production or abstract of such settlement, or any other explanation relating thereto, be required. But as to a term of 500 years that was limited by such settlement for raising £20,000 for the portions of the younger children of Sir Roger, and referred to in his said will, and as to a term of 1000 years which was limited by him in his will for providing for such children additional portions and annuities for unmarried daughters, the subsequent surrender or assignment of such terms respectively shall be deemed conclusive evidence of the payment of such respective portions, and of the release of or determination and satisfaction of such annuities. Various incumbrances were created by the late Sir Thomas and Lady Champneys of her ladyship's life interest in the estates devised by Sir R. Mostyn. The documents relating thereto, and other documents as to mortgages made by Mr. Mostyn on other estates than those in these particulars will not be abstracted, but any purchaser shall be entitled, at his own expense, to production or abstracts of such documents and mortgages not so abstracted, although the same may be occasionally referred to in the abstracted documents. Each purchaser shall bear the expense of examining and comparing the abstract with the documents of title, wheresoever the same may be.

Table showing the Fine to be paid for Renewing a Lease for 75 years, when part of the Term is expired.

Years expired.	Years Purchase. Common Fractions.	Years expired.	Years Purchase. Common Fractions.	Years expired.	Years Purchase. Common Fractions.	Years expired.	Years Purchase. Common Fractions.
1	1-20th	20	3-4th	39	2 7-10th	58	7 7-10th
2	1-16th	21	4-5th	40	2 6-7th	59	8 1-20th
3	1-14th	22	9-10th	41	3 1-50th	60	8 2-5th
4	1-12th	23	24-25th	42	3 1-5th	61	8 3-4th
5	1-10th	24	1 1-25th	43	3 3-8th	62	9 1-9th
6	1-8th	25	1 1-8th	44	3 3-5th	63	9 1-half
7	1-7th	26	1 1-5th	45	3 4-5th	64	9 6-7th
8	3-16th	27	1 3-11th	46	4	65	10 1-4th
9	1-5th	28	1 3-8th	47	4 1-4th	66	10 2-3rd
10	1-4th	29	1 9-20th	48	4 1-half	67	11 1-11th
11	3-10th	30	1 4-7th	49	4 4-5th	68	11 4-7th
12	1-3rd	31	1 2-3rd	50	5 5-10th	69	12 1-50th
13	2-5th	32	1 4-5th	51	5 2-5th	70	12 4-7th
14	7-16th	33	1 9-10th	52	5 7-10th	71	13 1-8th
15	1-half	34	2 1-33rd	53	6 1-25th	72	13 3-4th
16	4-7th	35	2 1-7th	54	6 3-8th	73	14 9-20th
17	3-5th	36	2 3-11th	55	6 7-10th	74	15 1-5th
18	2-3rd	37	2 2-5th	56	7 1-33rd	75	16
19	7-10th	38	2 2-7th	57	7 3-8th		

Again,—

To renew after 20 years have expired, look for figure 20 in the third column, and opposite this is the fraction ¾. If the rental be £40, divide the sum by ¾. Thus:—

	£	s.	d.	
¾)	40	0	0	Rental.
Amt. rqd. for renewal	£30	0	0	

And, again,—

To renew after 63 years have expired, look for figure 63 in the seventh column, and opposite this is 9½f. which means 9½ years' rent. If the rental be £20, multiply the same by 9½. Thus:—

Rental per annum, £20 by 9½ – £ 90.

EXPLANATION.

To renew after 10 years have expired, look for figure 10 in the first column, and opposite this is the fraction ¼. If the rental value be £10, divide the sum by 4. Thus:—

	£	s.	d.	
4)	10	0	0	Rental value.
Amt. req. for renewal	£2	10	0	

Figure 22

Building Regulations, according to the Plans to be produced at the Sale.

Levels of Streets.—That the levels of every new street shall be fixed by the vendor, or his surveyor for the time being, and every person who shall intend to make any new street, whether as a public way or not, shall give notice of such intention fourteen days before the commencement of such work; and every such person shall leave with the vendor a plan, drawn to a scale of not less than one inch to every ten feet, and the levels so fixed shall thereafter be kept.

New Streets.—No street shall be made without the consent of the vendor in writing; that being obtained, it shall not be lawful to form, lay out, or build to any new street, unless the same, being a carriage road, shall be, at least, thirty-six feet wide, and have a clear space for the bed of the street of not less than twenty four feet in width, with a sufficient footway on each side thereof, of not less than six feet in width, clear of any steps, or other projections; and in like proportion for streets of greater width.

Back Streets.—That any streets being an approach to the back of any house in any other street, and in which back street there shall not be the principal or only entrance to any dwelling-house, may be of a width of not less than eighteen feet, if a carriage way, and have a clear space of ten feet for the bed of the street, with a sufficient footway on each side thereof of not less than four feet in width, clear of any steps or other projections.

Height of Houses.—No dwelling-house shall be built in any street which shall exceed in height the width of the street, and that the height of any house shall be taken from the level of the ground floor to the eave of the roof.

Court Houses.—No court or court houses will be permitted to be erected for habitation.

Cellars.—No cellar shall be let as a distinct or separate habitation.

Passages.—No passage at the back side of any house or houses shall be formed of a less width than four feet; which shall be well and sufficiently, to the satisfaction of the vendor, flagged and channelled by the owner or owners of such house or houses.

Ashpits, &c.—No house shall be built without there being constructed, to the satisfaction of the vendor, in such situation as shall be appointed, a privy and ashpit, with proper doors and coverings to the same.

Coal Vaults, &c.—That no vault, arch, or cellar, shall be made under any street without the written consent of the vendor, and that all vaults, arches, and cellars, shall be substantially made, so as not to interfere or communicate with any drains or sewers; and if any vault, arch, or cellar, shall be made without such written consent, then it shall be lawful for the vendor to cause the same to be filled up or demolished.

Size of Rooms and Height of Stories.—No house shall be built which shall not have at least one room on the ground floor containing one hundred and forty-four feet, superficial, clear of any stairs, or staircase, or any other reduction whatever, save one chimney breast and fireplace therein; or which shall have any living room therein which shall be less than eight feet in height, or any bed-room less than seven feet six inches, save in attic-rooms, in which there shall be at least a clear height from the floor to the ridge tree of eight feet, such room or rooms, to contain at least eighty superficial feet, and no part of such measurement shall be taken from any point which shall be less than three feet perpendicular from the surface of the flooring board to the under side of the spars. No room shall be considered an attic room unless some part of such room is higher than the spring of the roof, and there shall in no case be more than one attic story. Cellars used as kitchens shall not be less than seven feet in height, and those not used for kitchens and habitation shall not be less than six feet in height.

Size of Windows.—Windows in rooms used for habitation shall be at least 5 feet 6 inches in height and 3 feet wide, clear of sash frames, or otherwise of an area of not less than 17 feet 6 inches, clear of the sash frame; those on the second, or bed-rooms, not to be less than 5 feet in height and 3 feet wide, or otherwise of an area of 15 feet, clear of the sash frame; and that the attic and cellar windows be not less than 3 feet square, or of an area of not less than 9 feet clear of the sash frame. And every such window shall be a casement window, opening on hinges or pivots, unless the sashes thereof shall be double, and made so as to open both at the top and bottom.

Plans.—Before beginning to lay or dig out the foundation of any new house, or to rebuild any house, fourteen days' notice in writing, shall be given to the vendor or his agent, by the person intending to build or rebuild such house; and every such person shall, at the same time, lodge duplicate plans and specifications with the vendor or his agent for approval, drawn to a scale of no less than one inch for every six feet, which shall show the house and outbuildings, the intended situation of the privy and ashpit, drains, the thickness of the walls, the strength of timbers, the height of stories, elevations, and an area of at least one foot wide and six inches below the bottom floor round the outside of the building, except round the yard wall, which area may be covered over with flags if preferred, care being taken that the entire space be left open under the flags, and that a grating one foot square be fixed in the flagging over every such cavity, so as to admit air. No house to be built within fifteen feet, at least, of the line of street, without special permission in writing, or without a flower knot in front. That the person so lodging the plans and specification shall not consider them approved of until signed by the vendor, or his agent, when one copy will be returned and the other retained. If such building be begun of, or made without such written consent, the vendor may cause such building or drains to be demolished.

Each Lease shall contain covenants by the lessee for himself, his heirs, executors, administrators and assigns, with the lessor, his heirs and assigns, for observance and performance of the above building regulations in such manner and form as the vendor, his heirs or assigns, or his or their counsel, shall think fit; and in addition thereto, covenants to pay to the lessor, his heirs, executors, administrators or assigns, a rateable proportion of the expense which the vendor has incurred or may incur in making the roads and drains thereunder and in lighting the roads; such expense to be certified by the surveyor of the vendor, his heirs or assigns, and also for contributing in a like proportion to all expenses of maintaining, repairing, and keeping in good plight and order, all such roads and drains and lighting apparatus; and also covenants to build in such manner as required by the above stipulations within *two* ~~one~~ year from the day of sale; and also covenants that all buildings shall be used exclusively for private residences, except otherwise permitted by the agent of the vendor, his heirs or assigns; and also covenants for periodical uniformity of outside stuccoing and painting, according to the direction of the surveyor of the lessor, his heirs or assigns; and for insurance against fire to the full value of the buildings for the time being, under the certificate of the surveyor of the vendor, his heirs, or assigns, in the joint names of the lessor and lessee, or their respective representatives or assigns in such office as the lessor, his heirs, or assigns may appoint, and also general covenants to repair on request; and likewise a covenant from the vendor for himself, his heirs, and assigns, to renew according to the scale hereunder written, and which is to be contained in a schedule to the lease, and generally such covenants for effectuating the present building arrangements as the vendor, his heirs, or assigns, or his or their counsel shall think fit, with a proviso for referring all questions, if any, which may arise on the provisions of such lease to arbitration in the usual way.

Figure 23

Examination of the Commissioners' records from the late 1850's reveals a regular pattern concerning the adoption of the roads prepared by the Estate. The Secretary to the Commissioners, John Williams, would first make application on behalf of the Hon.T.E.M.Lloyd Mostyn for certain roads or sections of roads to be "taken to". These would then be referred to the Surveyor whose inspection report and recommendations were available a short time later. It was by no means unusual for some further work to be required before the eventual "taking to" and adoption of the road or street as a public highway.

The records examined reveal the following:

1856 Parts of Mostyn Street and Church Walks.

1857 Part of Mostyn Street.

1858 North and South Parades.
Parts of Church Walks and Vaughan Street.
Conway Road (from Mostyn Street to the turning to Brynia Farm)

The last named was of great significance as it completed the new approach to Llandudno from Conway. It removed the necessity to follow the old parish road along the foreshore and up Nantygamar as described in a previous chapter. The construction of the Conway Road had commenced some years earlier and it was no doubt in general use some little time before its final "taking to" in June 1858.[91]

1859 Parts of Marine Parade.
Lloyd Street (from St.George's to Madoc Street).
Madoc Street (from Lloyd Street to Gorsedd Cottages).
Llewelyn Street (from Mostyn Street to Church Walks).
Clonmel Street (from Queen's Hotel to Mostyn Street).

1860 Mostyn Street (now complete from Church Walks to Vaughan Street.)
Gloddaeth Street from Mostyn Street to Madoc Street.
(Note that Chapel Street is not yet named and is thus a continuation of Madoc Street.).
Tudno Street.
Part of the Crescent.

1861 Part of Abbey Street.
A new street from the end(!) of Gloddaeth Street to Abbey Street (i.e. Clement Avenue).
Ty Gwyn Road.
Hendafarn Road.
Cwlach Road.
North Madoc Street from Gloddaeth Street to Tudno Street (i.e. Arfon Avenue).

The rapid increase in the numbers of buildings and streets of Llandudno was such as to necessitate the continual extension of the Sewerage System, from almost as soon as the main scheme had been

91 Whilst the route to Conway was thus much improved it was still necessary to negotiate the hills between Llanrhos and the river estuary at Tywyn. A further improvement in the communication with Conway was already under consideration in the form of the Turnpike Road Bill of 1856 which had the support of the Commissioners. This would follow a less hilly route from the Conway Bridge causeway towards Marl and Bodysgallen before passing to the east of Llanrhos and then joining Llandudno's new Conway Road. However, this did not happen and its need was greatly lessened by the arrival of the railway branch line. It is of course noteworthy that the proposed turnpike road followed the route now taken by the major portion of the recently constructed A470.

completed. There are records of numerous small schemes being put out for tender (e.g. in October 1858 the Mostyn Crescent sewerage extension was estimated at £32-1-4 but with a tender of £28-1-0 being accepted) and such works do not seem to have caused any major problems. In the case of the Madoc Street sewerage extension (originally estimated at £42-18-0) there was negotiation between the property owners and the Commissioners as to the location of the work to be done, with the former offering to pay any necessary extra cost for the works to be located in the back streets rather than the street itself. In the event the tendered cost for this modified scheme was £55-13-2, necessitating a contribution of some 10s from each house, and again there seem not to have been any major problems.

Our picture of the roads and streets of Llandudno which had been completed and adopted by mid 1861 is thus clear (see figures 24 & 25). It includes much of central Llandudno as we now know it and we must marvel at the enterprise and enthusiasm which had brought the new town into being in such a short space of time. Beyond argument it was a town which now bore much evidence of the Mostyn influence, not least being that of the names of the newly created streets. Names with family connections which had been used included not only the obvious ones of Gloddaeth, Mostyn, Lloyd, Vaughan and Llewelyn, but also that of Clonmel. The Hon.Edward Mostyn Lloyd Mostyn (by now the second Baron) had married in 1827, Lady Harriet Margaret Scott, a daughter of the 1st.Earl of Clonmel. In turn, their elder son the Hon.T.E.M.Lloyd Mostyn was mar-

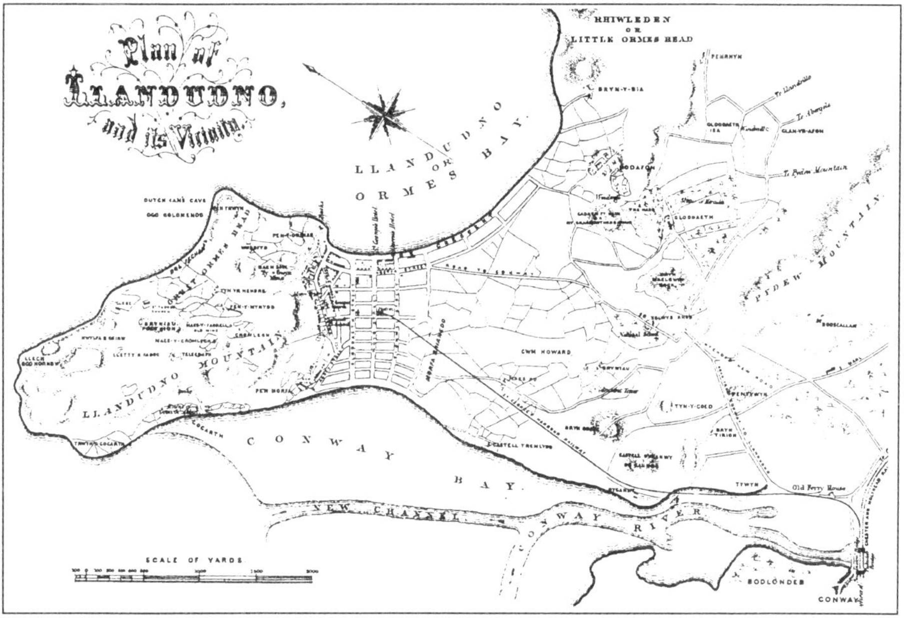

Figure 24

A visitors map of the late 1850's showing the anticipated grid system of roads. Note that it shows the railway station as in Lloyd Street, on the present lifeboat station site.

ried in 1855 to Lady Henrietta Augusta Nevill, who was later to have two of her own names used in the town, for Augusta Street and Nevill Crescent.

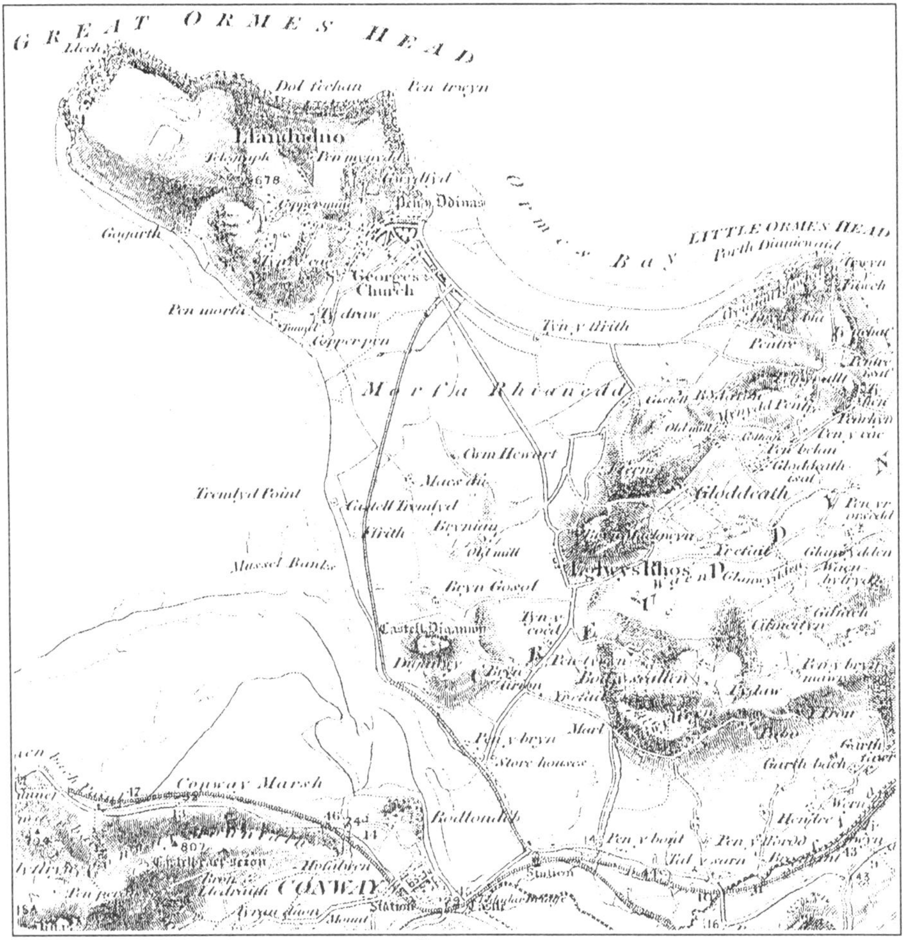

Figure 25
The ordnance survey map of the early 1860's, with its accurate representation of the roads present

The Llandudno Improvement Commissioners were concerned with matters of regulation of the resort from the earliest days. A bye-laws sub-committee was formed in August 1854 and its recommendations concerning Hackney Carriages, Horses, Donkeys, Bathing Machines and Boating were agreed in the following February and approved by Caernarvon Magistrates in April, well before the 1855 season. In the same period it was realised that there was the need for a Pinfold for straying animals and a site at Rofft Bach had been prepared. Consideration had next to be given to the appointment of a person to enforce the regulations (see figure 26 for a selection of paragraphs from the bye-laws).

It is relevant here to consider the general situation in the country and in the County of Caernarvonshire regarding policing at this time, for in the 1850's things were totally unlike those of the present day. It was only in 1829 that the Metropolitan Police was founded and it was in 1835 that boroughs were compelled to establish Police Forces. In 1839 an Act permitted Counties to do the same but not all did so as it was not made obligatory. It was not until the Counties and Boroughs Police Act of 1856 that it became so, and it was this Act

EXTRACTS FROM THE BYE-LAWS

FOR THE REGULATION OF BATHING MACHINES FOR HIRE, WITHIN THE LIMITS OF THE LLANDUDNO IMPROVEMENT ACT.

That licenses be granted (by the Commissioners) to authorise the owner or owners of bathing machines, and all persons employed by him, her, or them for that purpose, to ply for hire on the sea beaches and sands in front of and within the limits of the said town, and at such place or places as are hereinafter mentioned; and that on any complaint being made by or against any owner or owners, attendant or attendants of any machine, before any Justice of the Peace, such owner or owners shall, on the request of any such Justice, produce and show his, their, or her license, under the penalty or forfeiture of a sum not exceeding forty shillings for every non-compliance with such request.

That the words "Bathing Machine for Gentlemen," or "for Ladies," as the case may be, and the name of the owner or owners of every machine, shall be painted conspicuously on the outside thereof, and that the number of every machine named in the license shall be painted on the out and inside of each door thereof; and that the owner or owners of any machine using the same without being so named or numbered, shall be subject and liable to the penalty or forfeiture of any sum not exceeding forty shillings.

That every machine shall be properly and substantially built with fluted or chequered floors, so as to let off all standing water; also, a hand-rope fixed thereto, not less than ten yards in length, with a cork at the end, and a signal flag at the top outside, for the use of bathers inside, to enable them to give notice to be drawn ashore, and provide for each bather two clean towels, not less than three feet by one foot nine inches; also a looking-glass for each machine, and bathing gowns for ladies; and shall be kept in all other respects in good condition and fit for the purposes of bathing, and shall be approved of by the said Commissioners, or the person or persons who shall be appointed by them, for the purpose of inspecting such machine or machines, and that the owner or owners of every bathing machine using any machine without such hand-rope shall forfeit and pay for every such offence any sum not exceeding forty shillings.

That if the owner or owners, or attendant or attendants of any licensed bathing machine or bathing machines, shall, at any time or times, when such machine or machines shall be used for the purposes of bathing, neglect or refuse to place such machine or machines in a sufficient depth of water, so as to prevent the bather or bathers therefrom respectively indecently exposing his, her, or their person or persons, then, and in every such case, and for every such offence, the said owner or owners shall forfeit any sum not exceeding twenty shillings, save and except in such cases when the tide and weather shall prevent such machine or machines being so placed as aforesaid.

FARES.

For one person 6d., and 3d. each additional person per head. Forty minutes allowed. (This rule does not prohibit machine proprietors from entering into contracts with any person during their license.)

Any owner of machine allowing gentlemen to bathe in the ladies' grounds, or ladies in the gentlemen's grounds, either together or separately, it shall be lawful for the Commissioners to revoke such owner's license. (The positions of the machines to be changed every Monday morning, so as to give each proprietor a fair chance at the end next the town.)

STANDS.—LLANDUDNO BAY.

From a mark opposite the entrance of St. George's Crescent east to another mark placed opposite to the entrance of Clonmel-street, for ladies only.

From a mark placed 150 yards east of Clonmel-street to a mark placed 150 yards eastward of Bay-street for gentlemen only.

That every person bathing in the sea without a bathing machine within the limits prescribed by these Bye-Laws, shall, for every such offence forfeit and pay any sum not exceeding forty shillings, nor less than ten shillings.

That every proprietor of bathing machines shall provide and keep ready for use upon his stand two life-belts, with a coil of suitable rope for each, at least fifty yards in length, and that each machine shall be numbered conspicuously, and that the attendant on every bathing machine shall in any case of any property of bathers being left therein, immediately deliver the same to the policeman on duty; and every person offending against this Bye-Law shall forfeit and pay for every such offence a sum not exceeding forty shillings.

Figure 26

which brought the Caernarvonshire Constabulary into being.[92]

Prior to the establishment of a police force in any given area, the system of law enforcement had been a parochial one. Each year at Easter the parishioners elected their Parish Officers for the coming year, including Churchwardens, Overseers of the Poor, Surveyors of the Highways and the Parish Constable. A man of the Parish had to be the Parish Constable in his turn. The duties were various, including the distribution of food to the poor at Christmas, moving vagrants and pregnant paupers on to the next parish, and other odd jobs including the catching of criminals and bringing them before the Justice of the Peace!

This centuries-old system had not been without merit in old rural Britain, within villages of relatively static population. However, with industrial change and greater mobility it had become obviously unsatisfactory and even in those areas where these were not major factors, the system had its faults. More often than not the Parish Constable would delay action until it suited him (he might be a farmer who was about to milk or harvest his crops) or he would demand payment or expenses from the person who had been wronged, if he was to pursue the matter.

An Act of 1827 was an attempt to improve the system's efficiency by empowering the Courts to pay the costs and expenses of prosecutions, irrespective of whether there was real evidence produced for the case. This was of course an incentive to every man to be his own constable and resulted in many ill-founded charges being brought, and so in 1841 it was decided that costs would only be paid if a prima facie case was established. Over much the same period there were also the establishment of Associations for the Prosecutions of Felons.

These were a sort of club which offered rewards for information leading to convictions, and there was eventually one in Llandudno.

The last attempt to make the Parochial System more effective was the Parish Constable Act of 1842. Whilst this stressed the traditional obligation of every man to be Parish Constable in his turn, it legalised the growing practice of paying another man to perform the duties, and it also allowed the Parishes themselves to pay a salary to their constables.

This then, was the state of affairs which appertained when the Improvement Commissioners turned their attention to matters of Law and Order and so in May 1855 the name of a certain John Davies was agreed as Inspector of Nuisances and Pinner, at a wage of £1 per week. Unfortunately he declined the post, which was subsequently advertised (at 18s per week) as for a Policeman to be Inspector of Nuisances and to take charge of the Pound. From the six applications received one Evan Davies was engaged and by 25th.June it is recorded that he was equipped with clothes, hat, shoes, stick, staff, handcuffs and waterproof cover. However, his tenure of the post cannot have been considered satisfactory, for on 7th.August 1855 he was given notice.

Davies's replacement as Inspector of Nuisances and Policeman was Edward Polin of Dwygyfylchi and he was to remain

92 'The History of the Caernarvonshire Constabulary 1856-1950' by J.Owain Jones. Caernarvonshire Historical Society 1963.

in the post for some 18 months, until the end of February 1857. His appointment had been facilated by an offer to the Commissioners by Mr.Westmacott, the Mostyn Trustee, to defray the expenses of the appointment, up to a maximum of 25s per week. Polin's appointment was at 16s per week, plus clothing and the use of the dwelling near the lockup in Tycoch Road.[93] With the onset of winter he was allowed an additional 1s per week for coals. Whilst it seems likely that Polin took over much of the clothing that had been originally provided for Evan Davies there is a record that in June 1856 the policeman's clothes for that year were to be purchased locally, from Evan Hughes's shop in Mostyn Street, with shoes from the cobbler John Roberts and hat and tie from Mr.Pritchard, the owner of a long established shop (see figure 27), who was also a Commissioner.

It seems probable that Polin's activities in connection with law and order enforcement were generally satisfactory, though they were not always appreciated by the local boatmen and others. He was instructed to summons one boatman (the owner of the 'Lark') whose licence was also revoked for carrying too many passengers. The licences of two others were not to be granted until there had been due apology made to both the policeman and a Board Member for insulting and insolent language, and there were, of course, no licences for owners of boats or bathing machines who let out on Sundays. Polin's reporting of unspecified 'nuisances' is also recorded, with no fewer than eleven of these in the Commissioners' minutes for 16th.October 1856. These included both of the two large hotels, three premises in Church Walks, two bakers, one butcher

Figure 27
Pritchard's Shop in Church Walks, about 1860

93 The location of the town's first lockup is stated by John Roberts in his Advertiser article of 19th.February 1910, as being "in Tycoch Road, just behind the 'Stowe', Church Walks."

and one draper. John Williams, the Commissioners' Clerk was instructed to take proceedings, unless these 'nuisances' were removed

It was also in 1856 that Mr. William Hughes of Conway became consultant to the Commissioners for all legal matters, and his opinion was to be sought on a number of questions over the next few years. The first of these occasions seems to have been at the end of January 1857, after Polin had given one month's notice, when the Clerk was asked to investigate the Commissioners' powers under the new Constabulary Act of 1856. Mr.Hughes's opinions on two matters are recorded, these being that the Commissioners could only swear in Special Constables if they were apprehensive of serious riots or disturbances, and also that a policeman might well be appointed to Llandudno as a consequence of the Act.

The year of 1857 appears to have been a transitional one for law and order in the town, with the start of the separation of constabulary powers from those relating to the bye-laws. Whilst a George Rees of Liverpool was appointed as Polin's replacement he stayed only a few months, until June 1857. By July the house by the lockup was occupied by the County Police, thus necessitating the increase of the wage of John Walters, the latest appointee of the Commissioners, to 22s per week. Shortly afterwards, the newly appointed first Chief Constable for Caernarvonshire, Thomas Parr William Ellis, recommended that a man be appointed to Llandudno at what was then a Police Sergeant's wage of 23s per week, and for several months there were two policemen employed. As Llandudno's population was now in excess of 2,000 the Commissioners were hopeful of the town's entitlement to both, at County expense, but this was not to prove so. When faced with a bill of more than £14 from the Chief Constable, the services of the additional officer were dispensed with.

It was in this transitional year of 1857 that the Inspection and Nuisances Committee was re-convened. The reporting and recording of nuisances continued, with that from the Baths establishment – sewage discharge on to the rocks below – being notable. In October 1857 the multiple post of Surveyor of Roads, Inspector of Nuisances and Superintendent of all Sewers was advertised and in November Thomas Roberts was appointed at a salary of £25 per annum. Again, this was a short lived appointment but his replacement in April 1858 by Thomas Parry was to bring more stability, for he remained in the position for almost two years. Thomas Parry was himself a Commissioner and so of necessity resigned from those voluntary duties upon taking up the paid post, which now carried a salary of £40 per annum. Whilst undoubtedly the greater part of his function was that of Surveyor of Roads, the hybrid nature of his appointment was further demonstrated by the addition, in August 1859, of the duties of Inspector of Provisions and Inspector of the Market Hall.

Whilst the separation of constabulary duties from those of bye-laws enforcement was not abrupt, this general pattern was now emerging, though with mutual support where necessary. In 1858 the Chief Constable relented in the matter of police allocation to the town, and two constables were allowed for the summer months. He also agreed to their assisting in the enforcement of the bye-laws, provided that this was not to the detriment of their other duties. The constables' help in this connection was acknowledged by the Commissioners, who agreed a gratuity to each of 5s for a quarter, later increased by a further Is per week. References in the Commissioners' minutes to Constabulary matters after this time become much less frequent and in 1859 are limited to the necessary drainage work done at the lockup early in the year at the Chief Constable's request, and to the later provision of a pair of policeman's shoes!

In the Spring of 1860 a new set of revised bye-laws were formulated for the town. Whilst, as before, these included regulations relating to Hackney Carriages, Horses and Donkeys, Bathing Machines and Pleasure Boating, there were additional bye-laws for the Market Hall and Fairs. Before their final confirmation at the Quarter Sessions in April, the proposals had been exhibited in the town and as a result some minor changes were agreed in order to take account of the few objections which were deemed to be valid. One such, related to the location and boundaries of the bathing machines for gentlemen and ladies, and resulted in the use of the words "or for any length, distance or situation which the Commissioners may from time to time fix, alter or determine." By such means it was no doubt hoped that there could be an avoidance of further complaints on the subject of nude bathing, which was quite customary from the bathing machines even though bathing attire was provided. One such complaint, relating to males bathing opposite Gloddaeth Crescent, had been made directly to the Hon.T.E.M.Lloyd Mostyn by a Dr.Coley as early as August 1858, and this was only one of many subsequent complaints. However, it would be some years before the bye-laws were to be adequately changed in order to further regulate such matters by the prohibition of nude bathing.

The post of Surveyor and Inspector of Nuisances was filled from March 1860 by William Brookes, who was one of ten applicants who had tendered for the post. The tenders stated the salaries required and these varied from £30 to £78 per annum. Brookes's appointment was at £40 per annum and there seems little doubt of his increasing workload, for in August 1861 John Jones was appointed as an additional Market Inspector. In the identification of nuisances he was to be greatly aided by the scientifically based observations of a local resident, Dr.James Nicol, who in early September[94] offered his free services to the town in the capacity of Officer of Health, thus commencing a long and valuable association. His report on the sanitary state of the town was produced a few weeks later and acknowledged with thanks by the Commissioners. The instructions for the ordering of half a ton of disinfecting powder which are to be found in the October 1861 minutes were presumably given as a consequence and indicate the continued and necessary concern of the Commissioners for the maintenance of a nuisance free environment within the developing town.

94 A Public Health Act (10 and 11 Vict. Cap 34 sec 12) is referred to in the minutes of 5th.September 1861, at which meeting the appointment was recommended.

From the start of Llandudno's development it had been very evident that a most important feature would be the esplanade which would eventually skirt the magnificent bay, in front of the several 'crescents' of hotels. This had certainly been recognised by Owen Williams in his original concept for the town, which left a wide strip of land between the shore and the building line. In the words of the contemporary guidebook[95]:- "The bay is skirted by the Marine Parade[96] along which are erected ranges of handsome houses, including two spacious hotels for the accommodation of visitors." The guidebook goes on to describe the presence of the carriageway with a verdant lawn, between it and the sea. This abrupt transition from esplanade to beach is of course not to be found today, and it played a significant part in the building of Llandudno before the railway arrived to the area. The vast amount of timber which was used in the erection of the hotels and houses was in the main brought in from Menai Bridge by sea. The baulks were chained together, towed by steamer to the bay and left on the beach from which they would be later hauled by manual labour. Bricks and other materials arrived by sailing smacks and it is recorded[97] that it was not an unusual sight to observe as many as ten ships beached at the same time.

The first houses to be erected on the sea front after the planning of the Parade were Nos. 2 and 3, St.George's Crescent, with Belmont House on the North Parade quickly following.[98] The purchase contract of the land for the St.George's Hotel was signed as early as 30th.October 1852 and a copy of part of this is reproduced (see figure 29). The construction of the St.George's hotel was commenced in 1853 and it was opened in August 1854. This prime site was where there had been sandhills of some prominence and had been purchased by Mr.Isaiah Davies (see figure 28), the enterprising locally born son-in-law of the licensee of the Kings Head Inn, in the old mining village. At the same time, another large hotel, the Queen's, situated at the other end of the same terrace, was under construction for Mr.Owen Thomas. The choice of these sites well illustrates the sagacity of these early developers. Illustrations of these two major hotels were soon to be found in the

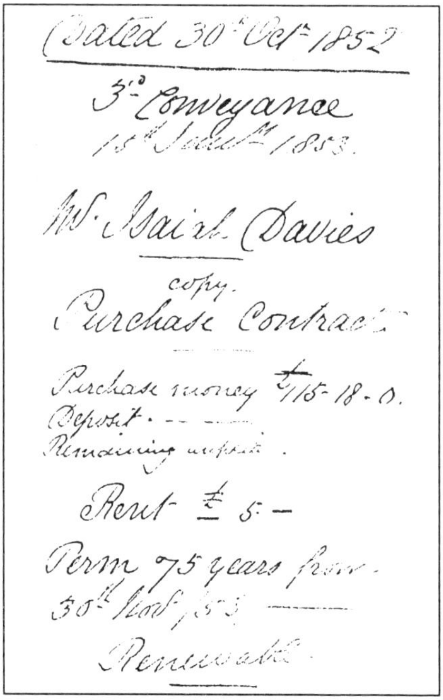
Dated 30th Octr 1852

3rd Conveyance 15th July 1853.

Mr. Isaiah Davies

copy.
Purchase Contract

Purchase money £715-18-0.
Deposit . -- --
Remaining unpaid .

Rent £5 –

Term 75 years from
30th Novr 1853 ———

Renewable.

Figure 28

95 'Hicklin's Illustrated Handbook of Llandudno'. 1858.

96 The word 'esplanade'was first used, but soon the use of the terms 'marine parade' and 'promenade' are also to be found.

97 Article in series 'Llandudno as it was' by John Roberts in Llandudno Advertiser issue of 19th.February 1910.

98 As 97.

local guidebooks, and have been reproduced in this text. It is, however, evident that not all of the proposals for very large hotels at this time were to come to fruition, for an 1860 document has been found relating to a proposal to form a company to construct the "Llandudno Grand Hotel", on a sea front site in the Eglwys Rhos parish.

There is no doubt that the sale of sea front building plots provided significant in-

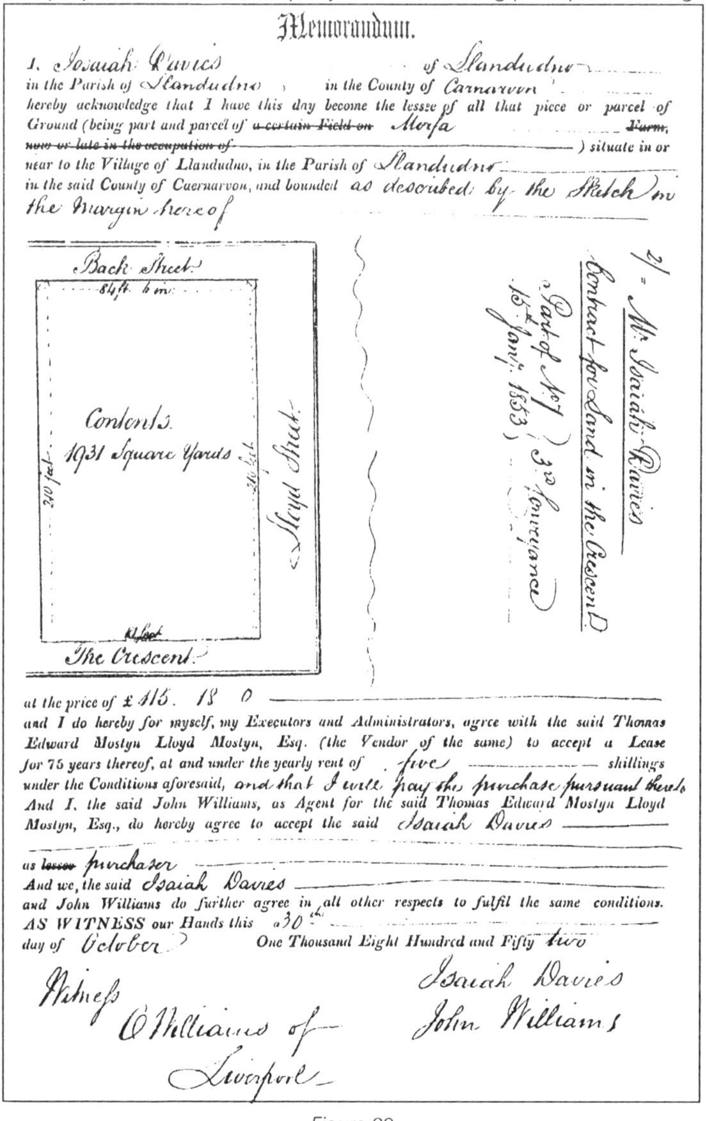

Memorandum.

I, Isaiah Davies of Llandudno in the Parish of Llandudno in the County of Carnarvon hereby acknowledge that I have this day become the lessee of all that piece or parcel of Ground (being part and parcel of ~~a certain Field on~~ Morfa ~~Farm, now or late in the occupation of~~) situate in or near to the Village of Llandudno, in the Parish of Llandudno in the said County of Caernarvon, and bounded as described by the Sketch in the Margin hereof

at the price of £ 415. 18 0

and I do hereby for myself, my Executors and Administrators, agree with the said Thomas Edward Mostyn Lloyd Mostyn, Esq. (the Vendor of the same) to accept a Lease for 75 years thereof, at and under the yearly rent of five shillings under the Conditions aforesaid, and that I will pay the purchase pursuant thereto And I, the said John Williams, as Agent for the said Thomas Edward Mostyn Lloyd Mostyn, Esq., do hereby agree to accept the said Isaiah Davies as ~~lessee~~ purchaser

And we, the said Isaiah Davies and John Williams do further agree in all other respects to fulfil the same conditions.

AS WITNESS our Hands this 30th day of October One Thousand Eight Hundred and Fifty two

Witness O Williams of Liverpool

Isaiah Davies
John Williams

Figure 29

come to the Mostyn Estate at this time (see figures 30, 31 & 32). The Gloddaeth, Mostyn and Neville Crescents were also soon to be developed, largely through the enterprise of newcomers from Birmingham, e.g. Messrs.Gwyther and Warden for Gloddaeth Crescent. Of course, as for all other carriageways in the town there was significant expenditure by the Estate in the necessary preparation of the road before its adoption by the Commissioners. However there was also the matter of the Esplanade (or Promenade) itself and the question of maintaining any sea defence work which might prove to be necessary. This latter question does not seem to have been a clear cut matter in these early days.

Figure 30
Gloddaeth Crescent, Llandudno

Figure 31
St.George's Hotel, Llandudno
Isaiah Davies, Proprietor

Figure 32
Queen's Hotel, Llandudno

It was in April 1855 that Mr.Westmacott attended a Commissioners' meeting, and, on behalf of the Hon.T.E.M.Lloyd Mostyn, proposed that the Estate would advance the necessary money for completion of the Esplanade, this to be repaid by the Commissioners from their anticipated later income from the rates. On the basis of plans by Wehnert and Ashdown, the total cost of this would have amounted to £547-15s-6d. However, at the same time the Commissioners were already involved with the sewerage scheme and whilst they expressed their gratitude for the offer, it was prudently declined.

It seems that for several subsequent years there was to be little significant expenditure on the seaward side of the carriageway. It was not until the Autumn of 1859 before the matter of restoration of the Promenade and the need for some permanent protection by means of a sea wall, was next considered by the Commissioners. By this time Mr.Westmacott's health was failing, and whilst he urged some action by letter, he was unable to visit Llandudno. It was the new Mostyn legal adviser, Mr.R.J.Cust[99] who suggested that the Commissioners had now superceded the Estate in responsibility for any necessary protection. An approach to Parliament should therefore be made, for the power to borrow money for any work that might be necessary, and the Estate would prepare any necessary plans and estimates.

As a consequence of this advice, a special meeting of the Commissioners was convened on 10th.November 1859, at which the Mostyn's local architect, George Felton, presented his plans, with an estimate of £5,800 for the works from the Baths to Tyn y Ffrith. The Felton plans were well received and he was complimented by the Board. Letters from Messrs.Cust and Westmacott made it clear that the Estate could not itself finance the work and that nothing would be done unless the Commissioners were to make the necessary moves. After a long discussion, Commissioner Chapman moved that notices should be placed in the London Gazette and other papers, of the intention to apply to the next Parliament, but there was no seconder and the meeting was concluded.

It is ironic that the late Autumn of 1859 was a time of violent weather and it was but six days later, on 16th.November, that the Commissioners allowed a sum of £10 for the use of labour to clear the Esplanade of debris in the aftermath of a violent storm. As has already been noted, this was the time of the virtual destruction of the first and short lived Llandudno pier. (There were however, sufficient remains of it still present in June 1860 as to cause the Commissioners to write to the St.George's Harbour and Railway company suggesting action because of the great complaints by visitors at the continuing unsightly appearance.)

The subject of a sea wall was next raised at the Commissioners' meeting of 30th.April 1860, with a proposal from Mr.Cust that the Estate could construct it as far as Ty Isa Road, if the Commissioners would undertake the continuation to Clonmel Street within 2 to 3 years. Consideration of this proposal was deferred for some time but by 11th.August 1860 it is recorded that a letter sent to the Hon.Mostyn stated that there was no intention on the part of the Commissioners to entertain the question at present .

The great amenity of the Llandudno esplanade was thus to continue to require attention at various times. There are numerous references to minor items of expenditure for its repair, including the authorisation of up to £20 in November 1860. At this time there was also to be some levelling of the Esplanade. A little later, in February 1861, notices were displayed exhorting the public to refrain from walking on the grass and in March there were further authorised repairs "using soil and Hayseed." At the same time, a gravel walk was "to be made along the whole promenade, using gravel from the beach."

Comment has already been made concerning the abrupt transition from Esplanade to beach at this time. This did present some problems in the late 1850's

99 Later to have his name used for 'Cust's Path', the precipitous walk around the Great Orme which preceded the Marine Drive.

and early 1860's due to the conflicting requirements of the local boatmen and visitors. The Surveyor was at various times instructed to clear the Parade of Boats, Poles, Nets etc. and also to ensure that only one end of a boat should be on the Promenade with the other on the beach. However, such inconveniences did not greatly detract from the visitors' enjoyment of walking in such close proximity to the shore and sea.

It was as early as 1857 that the first of the approved attractions for visitors was permitted on the Marine Parade. On 13th.August 1857 there is a record that written permission was given to the German Band then in the town, to play on the Parade for the amusement of visitors. A similar disposition to a German Band (perhaps the same one?) was to be given earlier in the next season, on 28th.June 1858, and we may thus conclude that the town's seaside brass band tradition dates from the very earliest days of the resort. It may be noted, however, that the Board did not consider it to be their province to be the providers of entertainment, for an application by letter from a Mr.Herbert Ellerby asking the Commissioners to do so for 700 excursionists was turned down in April 1859.

Figure 33
The cliff walk which became known as Cust's Path

The Caernarvonshire 'Pocket Companion' of 1792 to which reference has been earlier made[100] stated that "The religion of the establishment prevails, though Methodism struggles hard to tread on its heels." However, there can be little doubt that religious feelings in Llandudno itself were at a low level at the end of the 18th.century.

The only dedicated place of worship was the ancient church of St.Tudno (see figure 34), inconveniently situated for the cottages of the mining village on the lower slopes of the Great Orme. Here, in 1800, very few – and sometimes none – of the villagers attended the Sunday services held there by Robert Williams, the perpetual curate of Llandudno. He had been nominated to the parish in 1795 by the Archdeacon of Merioneth, who was the sinecure rector of the parish by right of the archdeaconry. Williams resided in Conway, there being no parsonage or other suitable house in the parish. It is recorded that in 1810 his emoluments totalled £32-10s per annum, well below that of Goldsmith's parson who was 'passing rich on forty pounds a year',[101] but this was to improve in the latter years of his long curacy, which lasted almost fifty years.

It is known that a few Baptists, the first of Llandudno's nonconformist groups, had been active before the end of the 18th.century, but by 1801 their small number had been reduced to one single faithful member, who walked to the meetings held at Fforddlas Chapel, near Eglwysbach. However, this situation was soon to change, for the spreading seeds of non-conformism were soon to make strong roots among the small community of miners and their families. A few Wesleyan Methodists were also active in Llandudno from about 1804, with the Calvinists only a little later, in 1806,

Figure 34
St.Tudno's Church, Llandudno

100 'Caernarvonshire. A sketch of its History, Antiquities, Mountains and Productions'. Author unknown but published for J.Debrett, Piccadilly 1792.

101 'Caerns Historical Society Transactions. The Nineteenth Century Parish of Llandudno', by Roger L.Brown.

though they were present earlier in other nearby areas such as Mochdre.[102] Shortly after this time, the Baptist cause gained more adherents.

This general increase in religious feeling was soon to be demonstrated by the construction of two chapels, that of Ebenezer for the Calvinistic Methodists in 1814, and the Baptists' Tabernacl in 1815. Both buildings were of course close to the old mining village, being respectively located in what are now Bodhyfryd Road and Upper Mostyn Street. Ebeneser was situated near to where the Clarence Hotel now stands and was leased from the Tynycoed Estate of William Jones at £1-1s per year. Spinther James relates that the Anabaptist Chapel was also built on Tynycoed Estate land, though this is contradicted by the fact that it is certainly to be found on the Mostyn Estate Schedule of 1843 (see earlier chapter on Llandudno before Inclosure). This discrepancy may possibly be explained in that it is documented fact that several portions of enclosure land were exchanged between the Hon.Edward Mostyn and William Jones and there may well have been other exchanges or sales in the previous decades.

It is known that at the time of building of these chapels the number of Wesleyans in Llandudno remained small, with several homes serving as meeting places over these early years. Most adherents evidently lived away from Llandudno village, in the Bodafon and Penrhynside districts. It was not until 1837 that the Wesleyans had their own chapel in Llandudno, this being Caersalem, in Cwlach Street, the premises being obtained from the Mostyn Estate at a rental of 10s-6d per year, this being shown in the 1843 estate schedule, next to the Baptist Chapel entry.

It is thus evident that allegiance to nonconformity was given by the majority of the residents of pre-enclosure Llandudno. That this was so is supported by the account of Thomas Rowlands which has been discussed in an earlier chapter, and which, somewhat to this author's surprise, contains references to the activities of the Mormons or Latter Day Saints. Though he was meticulous in his omission of any member of the Anglican Church, his account includes the great majority of the notable inhabitants of the village. It is also evident that non-conformism proceeded hand in hand with abstinence, for it is recorded that in 1835 the Llandudno Temperance Society had a membership of 250, or approximately one-third of the population.

The Anglican cause was not, of course, a lost one, and was indeed partaking in the religious revival. The swift replacement of St.Tudno's Church, which had been devastated by gales in 1839, by the St.George's Church (see figure 35) in 1840, was made possible by the generosity of the Worthingtons, the lessees of the Old Mine. At the time the 450 seats provided in this new church must have seemed very much an overprovision but within two decades the congregation would be numbered in hundreds and a further new Anglican Church would be in the course of planning! The foresightedness of building on this scale was indeed remarkable, for in 1840 there were no plans for Llandudno as a fashionable watering

102 A general account of the early years of non-conformism in Llandudno is to be found in 'Ebeneser, a story of Llandudno and one of its churches' by Rev.J.Roger Roberts. 1975. Photoprint Services of Conway. A more detailed account is in a series of articles entitled 'The History of Llandudno' which appeared in the Llandudno Advertiser in the Spring and Summer of 1925. These were based on the MSS of the late Dr.Spinther James.

place! It was at this time that Llandudno's first parsonage was built, on land given by the Mostyns, enabling the perpetual curate, Robert Williams, to take up residence in his parish for the last years of his life.[103]

It is of interest to contrast the lack of religious buildings and the low level of religious enthusiasm of 1800 with the situation of the early 1860's after the remarkable early surge of building in the new resort. There had been a flurry of church and chapel building coinciding with the increasing religious fervour of the late 1850's, with the result that virtually all of the possible religious requirements of Llandudno's population, both permanent and transient, could be catered for.

For the Baptists, their original Tabernacl in Upper Mostyn Street/ Llewelyn Street had been replaced by a new chapel on the same site in 1835 and joined by a sister church, Horeb, built higher up the Great Orme in 1860. The recorded congregation on one Sunday in 1851 in Tabernacl was as high as 190. In the 1850's the Baptists were also holding English language services and as a consequence the imposing Zion English Baptist Chapel was erected in 1862, on a prime site in Mostyn Street, leased from the Mostyn Estate. This seated 400 and remained as a prominent feature in the town until 1967, on the site now occupied by the Victoria Centre.

The Welsh Wesleyans' use of Caersalem had continued, with its rather slower increase in numbers. (In 1851 a congregation of 73, though a further 100 were at Moriah, Penrhynside). Again, a need for English Language services was develop-

Figure 35
St.George's Church, Llandudno
Published by Catherall & Prichard, Chester

103 'Caerns Historical Society Transactions. The Nineteenth Century Parish of Llandudno', by Roger L.Brown

ing and a temporary English Methodist Chapel was erected in Lloyd Street in 1861. This was vacated in 1866 with the construction of St.John's Church on another prime site in Mostyn Street, leased from the Mostyn Estate. The Lloyd Street site was later to be used for Ebeneser, the eventual larger chapel of the Welsh Wesleyans. (Note that the name Ebeneser was used at different times by both the Calvinists and Wesleyans. See Appendix.)

The Welsh Calvinists, with increasing congregations (over 150 in 1851) in Ebeneser Chapel which had been rebuilt and enlarged in 1837, built a much larger chapel, Seilo, in 1861. This was situated in Gloddaeth Street, close to where Ebeneser had been, and was on the site where the newer Seilo building now stands as the Welsh Presbyterian Church.

By this time the diversity of non-conformist religious provision within the town had further increased, and now also included the Independents, or Congregationalists. Christ Church (see figure 36) in Tudno Street was opened in 1857 and enlarged in 1863. Both English and Welsh services were held and it was planned that

Figure 36
Congregational Church

there should eventually be more than 900 sitting places.[104]

At this early stage of the town's development the Roman Catholic presence in Llandudno was still very small. However, in 1867 a building in Ty Gwyn Road was adapted for both worship and accommodation for a priest.[105]

In order to complete the picture at this time it is necessary to return again to a consideration of the Anglicans. As already has been stated, the new St.George's Church, though unexpectedly large, was already under great strain by the late 1850's.[106] There were as many as four services each Summer Sunday, two in Welsh and two in English. Two other Sunday services were held in the adjacent schoolroom, and arrangements were later made for services to be held in the St.George's Hall in Mostyn Street. All these were in addition to the Sunday services being held in the Church of St.Tudno, which had been restored in 1855 at the expense of William Henry Reece, one of the wealthy incomers to the town. Rowlands explains that this was in thanks for the recovery of his gravely ill daughter, under the influence of the pure air of Llandudno. Whilst this was undoubtedly a great benefaction to the town, it is of interest to speculate that perhaps one further reason for restoration had been the 1854 correspondence between the Improvement Commissioners and the then Secretary of State, Lord Palmerston. This had resulted in the order that for the protection of public health no new burial grounds should be opened in Llandudno without previous approval and that burials should be wholly discontinued at St.George's Churchyard. The consequent resumption of St.Tudno's Churchyard as the only burial ground in the area may well have given impetus to the restoration plan and will certainly have aided the general welcome given to its completion.

It was the Rev.Edward Thomas Evans who first drew attention to the increasing needs of English visitors. His role as a Commissioner and an early purchaser of plots in Church Walks has already been referred to, as has his death in Rome in 1857, when Chairman of the Commissioners. However, it was his successor, the Rev.John Morgan, incumbent from 1857 to 1885, who envisaged a new church with a much larger capacity than that of St.George.

At a meeting held in June 1859, a large committee led by Lord Mostyn and the Hon.T.E.M.Lloyd Mostyn was elected to raise funds to develop the project, which at that time was provisionally costed at £7,000 for a church to seat 1,200. The Mostyn family made a gift of land for the purpose, near to the parish boundary, but central to the developing town. Although the Hon.T.E.M.Lloyd Mostyn was to die tragically early, even before the start of the building project, his widow Lady Augusta Mostyn gave continuing support. Following both public and private subscription, building of Holy Trinity Church was commenced in 1865. The lower part of Mostyn Street was thus soon to be graced by no fewer than three imposing churches, these being Zion, St.John's and Holy Trinity.

---

104 For a description of all places of worship in Llandudno in 1865 see the Williams guide for that year.

105 An account of the growth of Catholicism in Llandudno is to be found in 'Our Lady Star of The Sea' by Margaret Amiel and Sr.Madeline Dunphy, published by Design 2 Print, Llandudno 1993.

106 See 'A History of the Parish Church of St.George and the growth of Llandudno' by Dr.B.G.Morgan F.R.Hist.S. 1990 printed by Colwyn Duplicating Services Ltd.

In turning next to the subject of the schools of Llandudno, the author will attempt to chronicle their development up to the 1860's, drawing in the main from the memories of Thomas Rowlands (written many years after the actual events described), certain newspaper articles and the early guide books for the town.

A few lines from the first source may be quoted with advantage.

"The first school I can remember was held in a small schoolroom behind Croesonen by a Frenchman, the father of the late Mr.Louis, the solicitor from Ruthin. Mary Ellen held another school in the Hen Gapel Bach.[107] Before long we had a British and Foreign School which was maintained by the Dissenters in the different chapels in turn.... There was also a small National School which is the present Infants School."

In his 1909 series of articles in the Advertiser entitled 'Llandudno as it was', John Roberts who had no doubt read Thomas Rowlands' book refers similarly to the Croesonen schoolroom and to the British School alternating between the Calvinistic and Baptist Chapels. In addition, however, he states that Thomas Parry, Ty Gwyn, kept a day school in a room near Tynypwll Farm.[108] There seems no doubt that his article attracted correspondence from its readers, for only a week later he writes that after further inquiry it seems certain that the first day school in Llandudno was at Ffrithcerrig; the mistress was one Mary Wynne.[109]

The limited educational opportunities in Llandudno in pre-enclosure days were thus provided by the initiative of both private individuals and the chapels. Rowlands states that the British and Foreign School was also attended by some miners in their spare time, and he speaks highly of the schoolmaster Williams, known to the local children as 'Schoolie Coch' because of his red hair. Unfortunately Williams' stay in Llandudno was not a long one and his successor was by no means as effective.

It was not until the 1840's that there were buildings in Llandudno which were specifically built as schools. These were the British School, now transferred from the chapels, whose building in Upper Mostyn Street was constructed in 1844, and the National school whose first building was opened in 1846. Information about them is contained in the early Llandudno Guidebooks, and it is evident that the latter, in particular, was held in high regard.

The first building at the National School was for 120 pupils and was erected at a cost of £500. However, in 1854 this became the Infants School, as a new school of 150 places had been added at a cost of £700. The buildings are variously described as being 'commodious and substantial'[110] and both 'neat and extensive'. The instruction was both 'moral and religious', by competent teachers under the superintendence of the incumbent, for this was, of course, a church school located near to St.George's Church and having the same name of St.George or Ysgol Sant Sior. In 1858 and for some years subsequently the attendances are reported as

107 A dwelling is named as 'Capel Bach' in the 1841 census, when it is occupied by William Owen and his family. It was perhaps one of the old meeting places.

108 Llandudno Advertiser 17th.April 1909.

109 Llandudno Advertiser 24th.April 1909

110 'This and other references in this paragraph are taken from Hicklin's Illustrated Handbook of Llandudno', 1858

about 100, with a further 80 infants, though in 1861[111] the only teachers named are a Mr.Hughes and a Miss George.

Examination of the Mostyn records shows that the land for the school was given from the Mostyn Estate to the Bangor Diocese. The conveyance was on 20th.November 1845 and was by Dame Mostyn Champneys and the Hon.Edward Mostyn Lloyd Mostyn, under the terms of the School Sites Act of 1841 which allowed for the free conveyance of land as a site for a school for the education of the poor.

As a footnote to this account of local educational developments the initiative of an earlier member of the Mostyn family must also be recorded. Miss Frances Mostyn (1748-1827), a daughter of Sir Thomas Mostyn the 4th.Baronet, and a long term resident of Bodysgallen, was noted for her benevolence and charitable acts. One such was the building and endowment of a school for boys and girls at Llanrhos, close to the parish church. This was opened in June 1822 and whilst it can obviously not be recorded as a Llandudno school, its close proximity to the developing town fully merits its inclusion in the account.

---

111 'Llandudno: Its History and Natural History'. R.Parry. 1861.

Whilst it was vital for Llandudno to provide the full range of places of worship needed to satisfy the religious fervour of the mid nineteenth century, it was also essential for the town to have some public buildings which could focus the activities and attention of the many visitors. Reference to early guides and other sources leaves little doubt that this need was appreciated and much publicity was given to the Baths, the Telegraph Station, the Market Hall and the Circulating Library facilities available.

That the provision of a public baths was essential for the new town's well-being had been early recognised. The views of Owen Williams were given in an 1848 letter to the Mostyn Agent, John Williams, in which he recommended the provision of "a baths at once, and a large plunge bath".[112] It was, however, not until seven years later, in 1855, that the Baths were built as a private venture, at a reputed cost of some £7,000. In the late 1850's at least one of the Improvement Commissioners[113] was a Director of the Baths Company, as was also the Mostyn Trustee, Mr.Westmacott.

The Baths building (see figures 37 & 38) was constructed to the design of Wehnert and Ashdown, the town planners for the Mostyns. Contemporary descriptions are fulsome in their praise of the establishment, which was situated on the site of the present Grand Hotel. It was both "commodious and handsome"; "a complete bathing establishment, with excellent private baths for ladies and gentlemen." Separate staircases branched right and left from the entrance hall, which itself led to an assembly room occupying the entire front of the building. This in its turn opened upon a spacious balcony giving "extensive and picturesque sea views." To the left of the hall was a library with beyond it a billiard room. There was also sleeping accommodation for the managers on the upper storey, facing the road. There was a steam engine with two sets of pumps to raise sea water from an extensive reservoir below, which was refilled at every tide.[114]

The unique position of the Baths as the only bathing establishment in Llandudno was soon to be challenged, with the opening of the Hydropathic Establishment on Neville Crescent and the Turkish Baths in Ty Gwyn Road. There was also the competition of the increasingly popular activity of bathing in the sea itself. It is evident that these several fee-paying establishments together comprised an overprovision, for by 1867 the last named had been sold at a considerable loss, when it was adapted as the first Catholic Chapel. By this same time it also appears that the Baths itself had changed hands at a fraction of its original cost and had suffered a period of suspension of operations, whilst the Hydropathic Establishment could at best be considered only a moderate success.[115] Matters were, however, to improve some years later with the building addition to the Baths Reading Room and Billiard Hall to become an hotel, and the Hydropathic establishment publicity emphasizing its worth as a winter residence for invalids.

112 This letter was referred to by Mr.J.Sutcliffe of the firm of Owen Williams and Sutcliffe in an address given concerning old documents held by his firm.

113 This was W.F.Chapman, a gentleman farmer who resided at Tebed Bryn-Maenol (now called Haulfre) on the slope of the Orme. His farm was Maesdu. Information in the John Roberts article in the Advertiser of 5th.March 1910.

114 See guides by Hicklin (1858), Parry (1861), Williams (1865) and Catherall (1866).

115 A general account is to be found in 'The Past, Present and Future of Llandudno', published in 1867 by Egerton Smith & Co., Liverpool, for the unnamed author who styled himself as F.S.A

Figure 37
The elegant design of the Baths is not quite equalled in the early photograph (see figure 38), which also shows Llandudno's first pier

Figure 38

In the 1861 Parry guide the Telegraph Station (see figure 39) is described in some detail, as occupying the highest location of the Orme's Head and commanding the most extensive of views. Reference is made to the signals "which pass on one side to Puffin Island, and on the other to LLysfaen." The Manager and his family are commended as civil and having a neat house and small garden, where visitors could be accommodated with refreshments of soda water, lemonade, ginger beer or tea, at a very moderate charge. It appears that a visitors book was kept, with entries for the visitor's name, profession and address. A nearby sheltered nook is described as a favourite resort for pic-nic parties. At this time the Telegraph Station was in its last years of operation for it was soon to be supplanted by the lighthouse with its electric telegraph equipment.

As has already been mentioned in an earlier chapter, the Llandudno Improvement Act of 1854 included powers given to the Commissioners 'for establishing and regulating a Market and Market Places therein'. The exercising of these powers did not prove to be easy, even though a Market and Slaughter House Committee was formed at the first (adjourned) meeting of the Commissioners in August 1854. In October of the same year an application was made to Lord Mostyn for a suitable site but the reply received was that this and other matters of siting would be duly attended to after the survey and plan of the town had been completed.

There is no further mention of this matter in the Commissioners records until a new Market and Slaughter House Committee was formed in April 1856, but its subsequent actions seem solely to have been concerned with siting of the Slaughter House. However, by August 1857 a Market Hall appears to have been privately constructed, for there is reference to the Llandudno Annual Sheep Fair to be held the next month in the enclosure next to the Market. That the Market Hall had been constructed by the Mostyn Estate Trustees

Figure 39
The Telegraph Station, Llandudno
Published by Catherall & Prichard, Chester

is confirmed by the record for 28th.June 1858 in which it is stated that Mr.Westmacott was willing for the Board to rent the Market (and the adjacent Pony Stand) on lease, so as to enable the Commissioners to exercise the powers of the Act. This was, of course, at a time of financial difficulty for the Board and so it was not until July 1859 that the Clerk was requested to write asking for the terms of such a lease.

The market buildings, which were stated to have been 'erected by Mr.Westmacott at the corner of Gloddaeth Street' were then leased by the Commissioners for three years from 1st.August 1859 at annual rents of £200 for the first year and £250 for the remaining years. In that same month, as already noted, Thomas Parry took over the duties of Inspector of Provisions and Inspector of the Market Hall. At the same time it was agreed that the opening hours for the Market Hall during the months of July to October would be from 6a.m. to 8p.m. and for the rest of the year from 8a.m. to 6p.m. except for Saturdays when the hall would remain open till 10p.m. By February 1860 the Commissioners had approved a set of Bye-Laws for the Market Hall and Fairs[116] and a little later in the same year estimates were obtained for the printing of the scale of Market Tolls.

A full description of the market building is to be found in the Hicklin Guide of 1858. It is stated to be "Opening from Mostyn Street into the main road leading to the Conway Bay", (i.e. Gloddaeth Street). The design was by Mr.Ashdown (of Wehnert and Ashdown) and the building's dimensions are given as length 102', width 52' and height at the roof centre 22'. There were sixteen stalls, some being sub-divided, with sixteen cellars or warehouses under. The description goes on to mention the nearby spacious range of livery stables and the stand for hiring ponies, donkeys, basket carriages and other conveyances.

Similar information concerning the size etc. of the market building is to be found in later guides. However we may then also read – in the Catherall publication of 1866 – that the Market Hall was then the property of a Company, though subject to the Commissioners' Bye-Laws. It is thus evident that the enquiries concerning the possible purchase of the property which were seemingly first made by the Commissioners in the late summer of 1861[117]opment see the minutes of the Commissioners for the years referred to i.e. 1858-1861. did not have a successful outcome, the result being the formation of the Llandudno Market Hall Company. However it is certainly clear from the literature available that the market and the adjacent 'pony stand' were an important area upon which the attentions of visitors could be focused.

When an examination is made of the fourth of the attractions which were regularly publicised in Llandudno's early days, namely the library facilities available, these are found to be surprisingly abundant. Mention has already been made of the library available at the Baths, constructed in 1855, but it seems unlikely that this was the first such facility.

Bartley's library is mentioned in the Commissioners' minutes of December

116 These are recorded as being largely the work of the Commissioners legal adviser, Mr.Hughes, and had shorter opening hours than those earlier agreed. It is a matter of amazement to the author that the Commissioners Market Bye-Laws were published in contemporary guides and mis-dated as applying from May 1854 – a date before the passing of the Llandudno Improvement Act and several years before the market was built. There are of course no bye-laws for the market in the 1858 guide.

117 For this and for other information concerning the market development see the minutes of the Commissioners for the years referred to i.e. 1858-1861.

1856, when they were informed that the proposed site for the Llandudno Railway Station would be in a field opposite Bartley's Library. Whilst Samuel Bartley's multifarious business activities are known to have been located in Compton House, Mostyn Street by 1861, (on the Lloyd Street corner site of the present Natwest Bank), he is known to have started in business in 1852 and the reference may thus be to some other, earlier, site. It is also possible that this accounts for the erroneous placing of the railway station in Lloyd Street in the visitors map given in the chapter on housing and streets (see figure 24).

By 1859 there are several other libraries which can be traced. Herbert Ellerby's Central Library was situated in Upper Mostyn Street whilst Mr.Bridge's Circulating Library was much further down, in the newer Mostyn Street area, which at this time had seen most of its development on the eastern side. Mention may also be made of William Powell[118] of the Post Office, who advertised as a Bookseller, and of Thomas Williams the Chemist in Church Walks. Amongst the latter's many enterprises was the publication every Saturday of the 'Llandudno Directory and List of Visitors'. This cost 2d and had been available since 1854.

Whilst it has been the general intention of the author to take his account of Llandudno in this first volume up to the end of 1861, a little latitude has been already taken in the case of the religious buildings and one further similar extension is thought to be relevant here. This concerns the St.George's Hall, the first building to be built "for holding of public concerts, lectures, literary meetings and other gatherings for useful instruction and entertainment." This impressive building, with a capacity of some nine hundred persons was constructed in 1864 on the west side of Mostyn Street and was to play a major role in the leisure activities of the town until the middle of the next century, though latterly as the Princes Cinema.

118 Llandudno's original post office was at Green Hill, Old Road, and was kept by William and Ann Jones. William Powell married their daughter and took over, afterwards moving to Llewelyn Street and later to Mostyn Street. The information is given in the Llandudno Advertiser 1925 in the series of articles based on the MSS of the late Dr.Spinther James.

Whilst a detailed historical study[119] from early times of the Mostyn manors of Gloddaeth and Bodysgallen has not been one of the aims of this account of Llandudno, their close proximity to the town has made some references inevitable. A few more such references will now be made, these being concerned with items which have aroused the author's interest in the course of his research.

Whilst some variation of place name spellings over the years is to be expected, that found for these manors is of remarkable diversity when compared with Llandudno, whose only variants would seem to be the Llandidno of 1643 and the later Llandydno.

For Gloddaeth (see figure 40), the following have been found: Clothiet (1494), Clothieth (1528), Glothaeth, Gloddeth, Gloddaith, Gloddedd, Glothaith, Glothaithe, Glothiaith and Glotheth.

For Bodysgallen (see figure 41), there have been a similar number of variants found, these being Bodschallen, Bodycallen, Bodycallan, Boduscallan, Bodsgallen, Bodesgallen, Boddescallon, Bodescallen, Bodeschallen, Bodyschallen and Bod y Skallen.

On the matter of the meaning of the place names it is suggested that Bodysgallen signifies the dwelling place of Caswallon[120] or, more fully, Caswallon-law-hir. (Caswallon long handed). A more mundane suggestion is that it is simply a place in the thistles. There are, also, two suggestions for the derivation of Gloddaeth, one being that it has a connection with glo (coal, perhaps charcoal) or cloddfa (mine), the other that it means the place of feasting or place of rejoicing.

The latter derivation would, of course, be appropriate, bearing in mind the famous hospitality of the Mostyn family, which has already been noted in an earlier chapter. There is further possible support for this in the knowledge that the Bard Lewis Mon mentions the 'wine presses' at Deganwy, indicating the presence of extensive vineyards in the neighbourhood.[121]

Whilst the bardic references to such feasting are from the distant past, similar accounts are to be found in the reminiscences published early in this century.[122] In particular, the tenants' rent dinner was for many years a special event at Gloddaeth, where it was held in the large reception hall. This is of no surprise to the author for in the research a number of references have been found to the considerate conduct of the Mostyns as landlords and employers. One notable example – that of the medical attendance upon all members of the households – has been recorded in the second chapter of this account, and a further striking reference is to be found in the will of an employee, dated 25th.November 1837.[123] This was that of Thomas Jones, a

119 If such is required, see, for example, the article entitled Gloddaeth by Constance Sutcliffe in the May 1896 issue of the Pall Mall magazine, or the Historical Sketch of Gloddaeth sold in September 1889 in aid of funds of the Llandudno Cottage Hospital at the Fete and Garden Party held at Gloddaeth, or the articles Gloddaeth and Bodysgallen by Richard Haslam which appeared in successive issues of Country Life dated 7th.and 14th.December 1978.

120 See, for example, the Glossary of Proper Names in the Parry 1861 volume on Llandudno

121 See 'Gloddaeth and Mostyn in the Olden Times'. An address by Rt Hon.Lord Mostyn, F.S.A., given in 1926 to members of the Llandudno, Colwyn Bay and District Field Club and reported in their proceedings for that year.

122 Accounts by John Roberts are to be found in the issues dated 24th.July and 31st.July 1909 of the Advertiser.

123 Mostyn MSS.No.8901 U.C.N.W. Bangor.

butler for the Mostyns, who, after a number of bequests to members of his family and fellow employees, left the residue of his estate to Roger Mostyn, second son of Edward Mostyn Lloyd Mostyn, who was aged 6 years at the time.

It is of interest to consider some of the occupants of Gloddaeth and Bodysgallen during the first half of the nineteenth century, the main period considered in this account. Whilst they seem to have been seldom visited by Thomas, the sixth Baronet (1776-1831), other members of the extensive family were residing in the area. Reference has already been made to his aunt, Miss Frances Mostyn (1748-1827) of Bodysgallen in connection with her endowment of Llanrhos School in 1822 and her further benevolence in repairing the parish church at Llanrhos is commemorated by a tablet in that building. His sister, Charlotte Margaret, as Lady Mostyn Champneys, resided with her husband Sir Thomas Swymmer Mostyn Champneys at Gloddaeth for much of the 1830's, after she succeeded to the life interest in the Mostyn Estates in 1831. As a widow, she is also recorded in the 1841 census, living at Gloddaeth with five servants. Two other unmarried sisters of this last baronet were also to reside at Bodysgallen, these being Catherine Mostyn and Mary Bridget Mostyn, the latter until her death in 1856. Again, they are both recorded in the 1841 census.

By the mid-1840's Gloddaeth was to become the principal residence of the Hon.Edward Mostyn Lloyd Mostyn and his family, until his succession to the Barony in 1854, and it was during this period of occupancy that his son Thomas – who was soon to be Chairman of the Improvement Commissioners – attained his majority. This was on the 25th.January 1851, and whilst there were doubtless family celebrations elsewhere, the occasion was to be

Figure 40
Gloddaeth
The Ancient Mansion belonging to the Hon.E.M.Ll.Mostyn M.P.

marked by two days of celebrations in the parishes in or near to Llandudno and Conway. It is recorded that children from no fewer than 13 nearby parishes were gathered together on the first day, with the assembly of many farm carts and wagons near to Llanrhos Church.[124] The colourful procession moved on to Llandudno where a feast was available near to the George and Dragon Inn. On the second day it was the turn of the adults of the same 13 parishes to take part in the feasting, whilst on the Orme some small explosive charges were detonated in celebration.

The census returns for 1851 were taken a little later than these celebrations, on the 30th.March. Their examination reveals the large scale of the staffing of the two manors. At Gloddaeth are to be found a Housekeeper, Cook, Groom, Coachman and no fewer than sixteen others listed as Houseservants. On the night of this census the Hon.Edward Mostyn and his five sons were all away, but his wife Harriet and their five daughters were in residence. Similarly, at Bodysgallen, though Mary Bridget Mostyn is absent, there are listed a Housekeeper and eighteen other servants, indicating an establishment of similar size.

Whilst the picture revealed by the 1851 census can be considered to reflect a certain greater stability in the Mostyn affairs, it must be born in mind that for many further years the estates were to remain subject to the direction of the trustees appointed as a result of the financial arrangements that had been earlier made.

Major changes in the occupancy of the manors were soon to take place, following the removal from Gloddaeth to Mostyn of the Hon.Edward on becoming 2nd.Baron in 1854, and the death of Miss Mary Bridget Mostyn in 1856. The family presence in the area was then much reduced, for though the Hon.Thomas Mostyn and his wife Lady Augusta were nominally in residence at Gloddaeth, his duties as an M.P. necessitated another residence in the London area. it may be noted that both of their sons

Figure 41
Bodysgallen Hall

124 See, for example, the description in the Parry 1861 volume on Llandudno.

were born in Portland Place and that the Hon.Thomas's last attendance at a Commissioners' meeting was in August 1858 (though Lord Mostyn attended one in May 1860). It is evident that the Hon.Thomas Mostyn was not a man of robust constitution and towards the end of the decade it seems that he showed evident symptoms of debility, which eventually caused his withdrawal from public life. At the time of his last illness, he was at Birling Manor, near Maidstone, a family home of the Earl of Abergavenny, father of his wife, Lady Augusta. The 1861 census entry for Gloddaeth Hall, made on April 7th., is a significant one, for it records the presence only of one Housekeeper and one Houseservant.

The Hon.Edward Mostyn Lloyd Mostyn died on 8th.May 1861, leaving his widow, Lady Augusta Mostyn, with two young children, aged 5 and 4. It would be some years before Lady Augusta returned to Gloddaeth to play her very major part in the life of Llandudno, and it was to be 1884 before her older son, Llewelyn Nevill Vaughan succeeded as 3rd.Baron.

The choice of the year 1861 for the conclusion of this first part of Llandudno's history was made for several reasons. The first, and most obvious reason, is that it was the year in which the Hon.Thomas Edward Mostyn died, at the early age of 31. His death added a further complication to the complex financial affairs of the family, for in 1852 arrangements had been made for his purchase of life estates of both his grandfather and father.[125] Whilst by 1861 his grandfather was dead, his father the second Lord Mostyn, was now 66 years of age and living at Mostyn. His son and heir to the title and estates was but five years of age, and with his younger brother and mother Lady Augusta, was now at Birling Manor. There was thus no Mostyn presence in Llandudno and the dealings of the Commissioners on all matters connected with the Mostyn Estate would be with the trustees, the most notable being Mr.Cust.

Though he had not attended any meeting of the Commissioners for several years, the Hon.Thomas Edward Mostyn had been, whenever necessary and in his absence, re-elected as their nominal Chairman. This non-attendance at Commissioners Meetings was not indicative of a lack of interest in the affairs of Llandudno, either on his own part or that of his wife. As an example of this interest it may be noted that with his father he headed the Committee which had been elected to raise funds for the proposed new Trinity Church. Again, as late as January 18th.1861, less than four months before her husband's death, Lady Augusta Mostyn had performed the naming ceremony at the launching of Llandudno's first lifeboat, the Sisters Memorial[126] (see figure 42).

The news of the Hon.Thomas Edward Mostyn's death was given to the Commissioners by John Williams at the meeting held on 13th.May 1861. Copies of the following letter were subsequently sent to both Lady Augusta Mostyn and to Lord and Lady Mostyn.

'It is with extreme and painful regret that the Board has received the sad and melancholy intelligence of the death of the Honourable Thomas Edward Mostyn Lloyd Mostyn M.P.

While the Board expresses its deep sympathy and condolence to the family it is also desirous to place on record the loss it has sustained in the lamented demise of the honourable gentleman who has always taken the warmest interest in promoting the improvement and prosperity of Llandudno and for years been unanimously elected one of the Town Commissioners and with so much ability courtesy and impartiality acted as Chairman of this Board'

The following reply from Lord Mostyn was reported on 27th.May:

'I beg you will have the goodness to convey to the Llandudno Improvement Commissioners my grateful acknowledgements for their sympathy and condolence on the occasion of my son's death'

A reply from Lady Augusta Mostyn is recorded in the Commissioners' minutes for the 6th.June meeting. It was sent on her behalf by R.J.Cust. the Mostyn Trustee, writing from Eccleston Square.

'I am requested by Lady Augusta Mostyn to acknowledge with many thanks the kind expressions of condolence which

125 Mostyn MSS.No. 297 at U.C.N.W. Bangor.

126 For a description of this ceremony see the Parry volume of 1861.

have been transmitted to her from the Commissioners of Llandudno. The late Mr.Mostyn had always taken a lively interest and pride in the welfare and prosperity of the town of Llandudno, and esteemed highly the honourable position which he held as Chairman of the Board of Commissioners, as well as the universal kindness and courtesy which he always received at the hands of the inhabitants of the town.

Lady Augusta Mostyn feels sure that this melancholy event will not diminish the kind and friendly interest which the people of Llandudno have always shown towards the family of Mostyn and she hopes that the time may come when her son may not only witness a large increase in the prosperity of the town, but may also renew in his own person those ties of friendship which have always united his family to the inhabitants of this neighbourhood.'

Whilst the author has allowed himself a little latitude in earlier chapters to follow a developing theme to a few years on, a further reason for the choice of the year 1861 is that it affords a convenient point for an assessment to be made of the development of the new town. In this context it cannot be over-emphasized that mid-1861 was only seven years after the appointment of the Board of Improvement Commissioners, and only twelve years after the first offer for sale of building land! The changes in this short space of time are well nigh unbelievable.

The Llandudno resident of 1849 lived in an unusually shaped parish of approxi-

Figure 42
Sisters' Memorial

mately 200 dwellings. Of these, some 170 were in the 'Upper Township' by the Great Orme, the rest being in the 'Lower Township' comprising the detached portion of the parish around Brynybia, Bodafon and Nantygamar. The latter was separated from the major portion of the parish by the parish of Eglwysrhos, which contained the farms of Maesdu, Brynia and Cwm Howard and the Tyn y ffrith smallholding. For a resident living in the village proper, most of his few necessary purchases will have been made at Pritchard's shop in Church Walks, then at the very heart of the village.

This picture may be contrasted with that to be found in 1861, when the population had more than doubled and occupied no fewer than 438 residences in the Llandudno parish. Of further significance, however, is the fact that though closely prescribed as to its possible area by the Improvement Act, the developing town was not limited to the confines of Llandudno parish. The developments at Mostyn Crescent and Neville Crescent were in Eglwysrhos parish, as also was Vaughan Street. A note relating to this point is to be found in the Surveyor's report given to the Commissioners on 7th.August 1860, which refers to the 'boundary of the Act at Tynyffrith', a smallholding within the Eglwysrhos parish (see figure 43).

Whilst the 1861 resident will still have looked to the Ormeside Church Walks area for a number of necessary facilities, including those provided by the Commissioners'

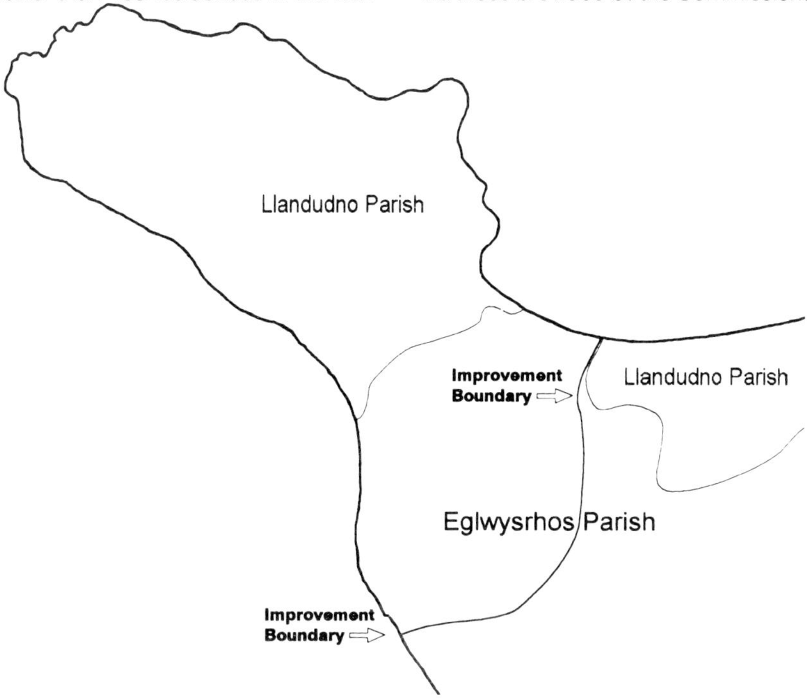

Figure 43
Improvement Area Boundary included Eglwys Rhos Parish townships of Tre Fferm, Tre Hir, Tre Cwm and also parts of Tre Gloddaeth and Tre Brynia.

Offices, the Gas and Water Offices and the town's first bank which was established in 1860, he would no longer be restricted to Mr.Pritchard's shop for his purchases (see figure 44). On his way down to the now thriving areas of Mostyn Street he could now call in at Thomas Williams' "Homoeopathic Depot" and "Italian Warehouse" (see figure) (housed in part of what is now the Empire Hotel) and purchase various

Figure 44

forms of pasta, a Westphalian Ham or even Reindeer Tongues. At Actons (see figure 47) he could buy good French gloves for his wife at 1s-6d a pair then walk past the thriving market and on to his tailor, John Davies, in Clonmel Street (see figure 48). On his return, after walking up the esplanade past the magnificent hotel crescents, he might take notice of the large van of Cornaby's Photographic Portrait Institution (placed on the land now occupied by the Carlton Buffet) whose 1861 advertisement proclaimed it to be now open for the fourth season (see figure 46).[127]

This latter picture of Llandudno life indicates a degree of sophistication which may well have seemed unreal to the indigenous older inhabitants. It was, however, necessary for the comforts of the thriving middle class who were now taking their holidays – often with a servant – in the resort. Their names had been recorded each week by the Llandudno Directory

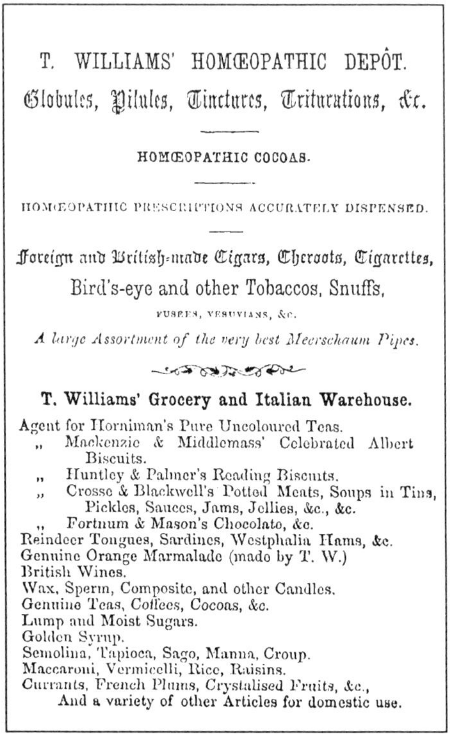

Figure 45

since 1854, and this was joined in 1860 by the 'Llandudno Visitor'.[128] Their interests reflected those generally held by the educated classes of the mid-Victorian era, and Llandudno's botanical, geological and artistic interests, together with its improved accessibility, magnificent seaside location, equable climate[129] and good hotels and

127 An account of the first photographers in Llandudno is to be found in John Roberts' article in the Advertiser of 4th.December 1909.

128 Information given by S. Wicklen.

boarding houses were providing them with what they wanted.

The situation for Llandudno in 1861 can thus be described generally as one of satisfactory, even remarkable, progress. Though there had been some false starts and major financial problems for them, the achievements of the Commissioners were indeed impressive. With the help and co-operation of the Mostyns, their Trustees and the Estate's employees, there were now roads and impressive buildings, gas and water services. These, together with the bye-laws and rating income necessary for the regulation and administration of an orderly town, had generated a situation which was attractive to outsiders and the town was rapidly increasing in size. The general plans for this expected further development had been laid, and the Commissioners under a new Chairman could look forward to this with some confidence. They would, of course, continue to have the presence of John Williams, the Mostyn local agent, as their Secretary, and would need to have the continuing co-operation of the Trustees of the Mostyn estate.

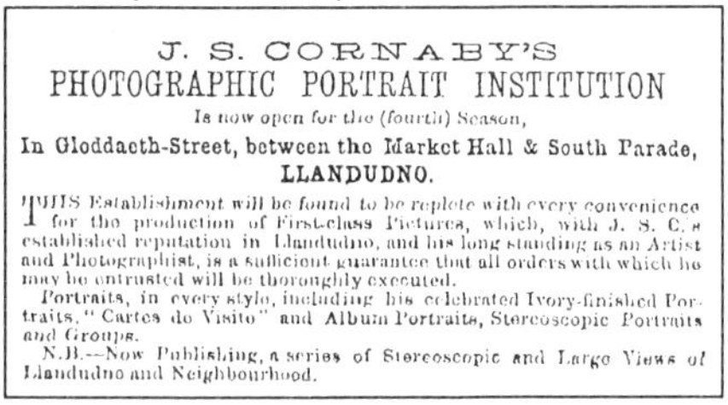

Figure 46

Figure 47

Figure 48

129 There are some remarkable descriptions of Llandudno's climate in the contemporary literature. Parry's volume devotes no fewer than 26 pages to it and Dr.Coley's Medical Guide for Visitors to Llandudno, published in 1859 devotes several pages to the subject before listing the numerous diseases "for the relief of which Llandudno is eminently adapted."

The Early Mostyns

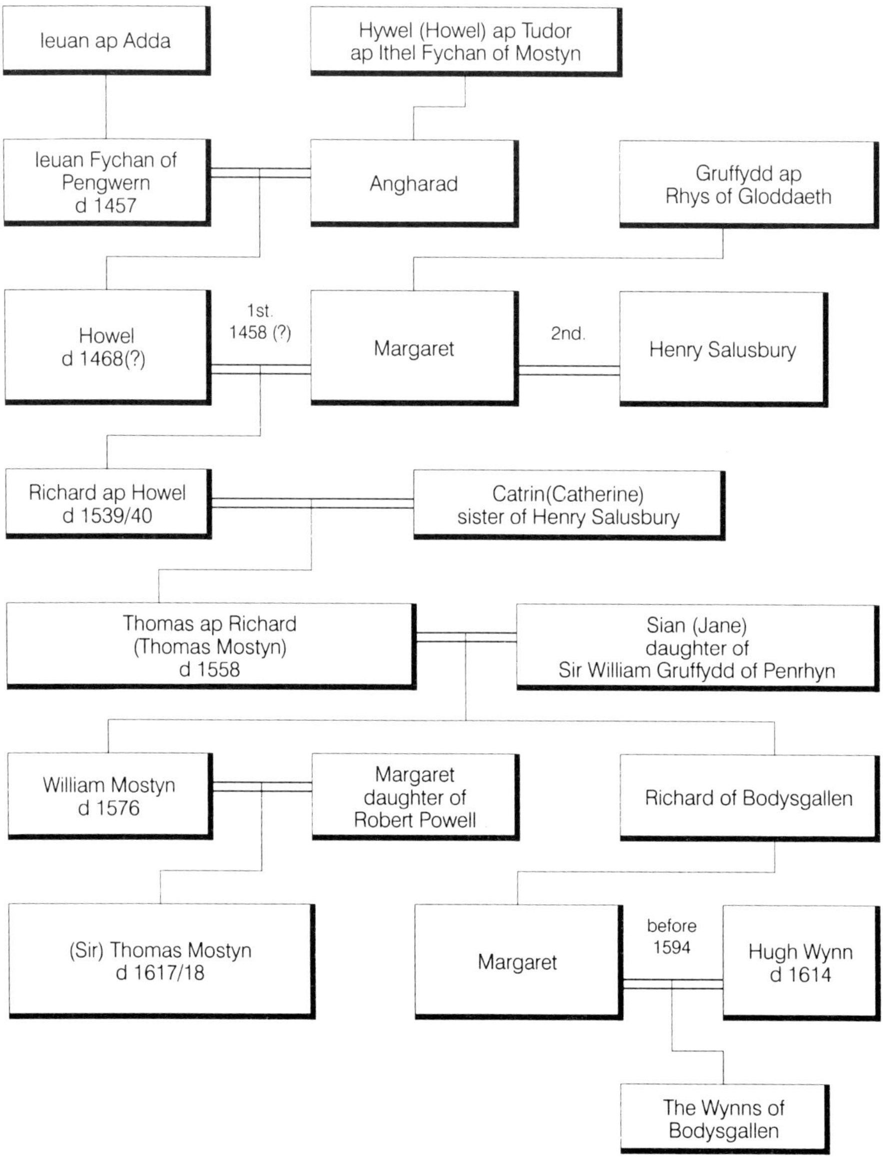

Key
b - born, **d** - died, **d unm** - died unmarried
dsp - decessit sine prole (died without issue)

The Mostyn Knights and Baronets

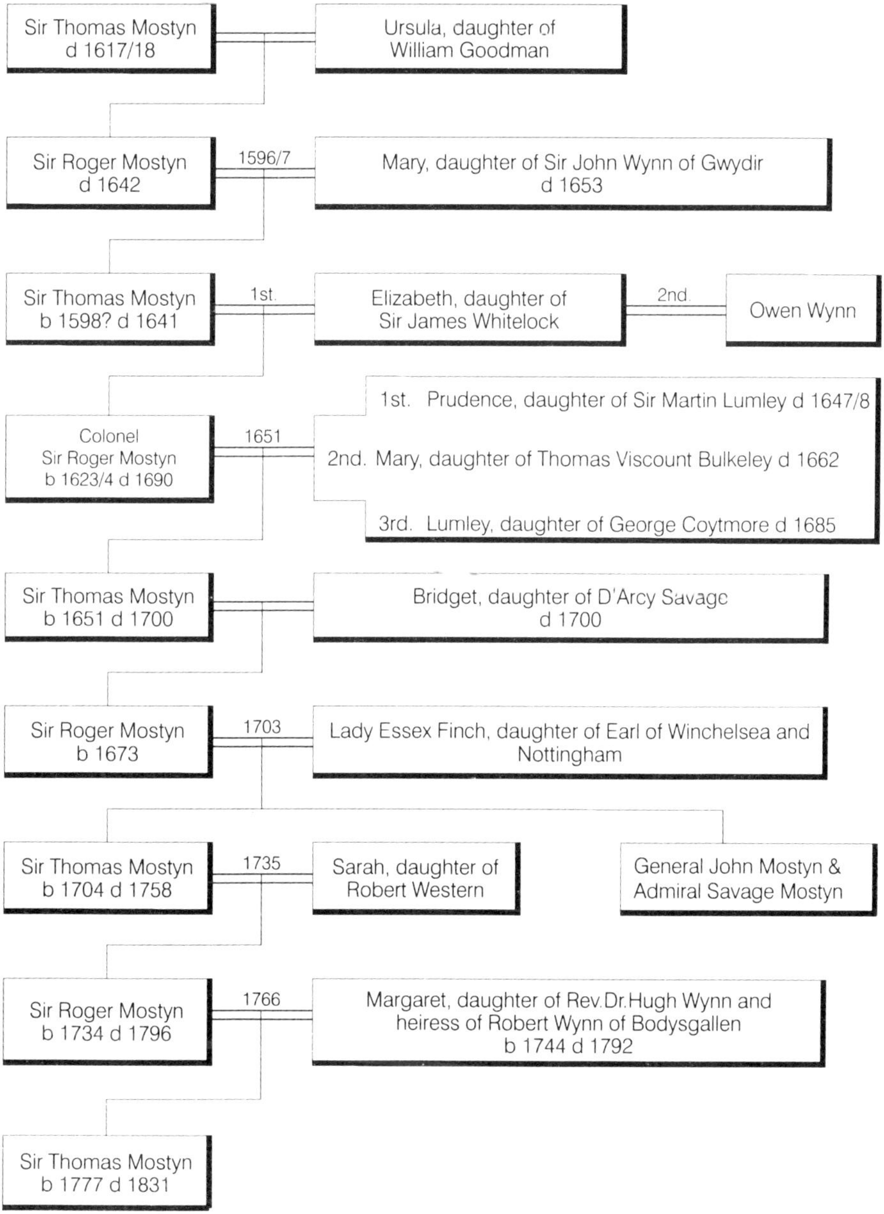

Key
b - born, **d** - died, **d unm** - died unmarried
dsp - decessit sine prole (died without issue)

The Lloyd Succession

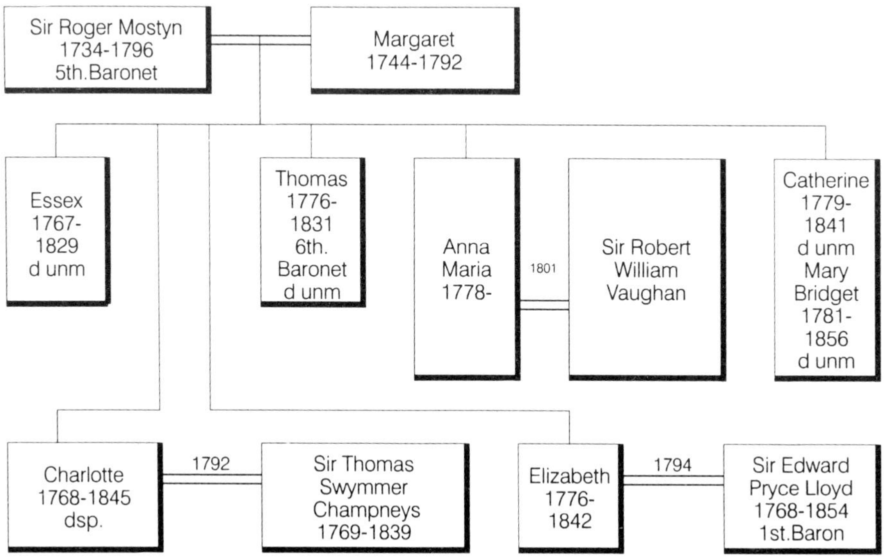

Key
b - born, **d** - died, **d unm** - died unmarried
dsp - decessit sine prole (died without issue)

The Lloyds at the Time of Succession to the Mostyn Title

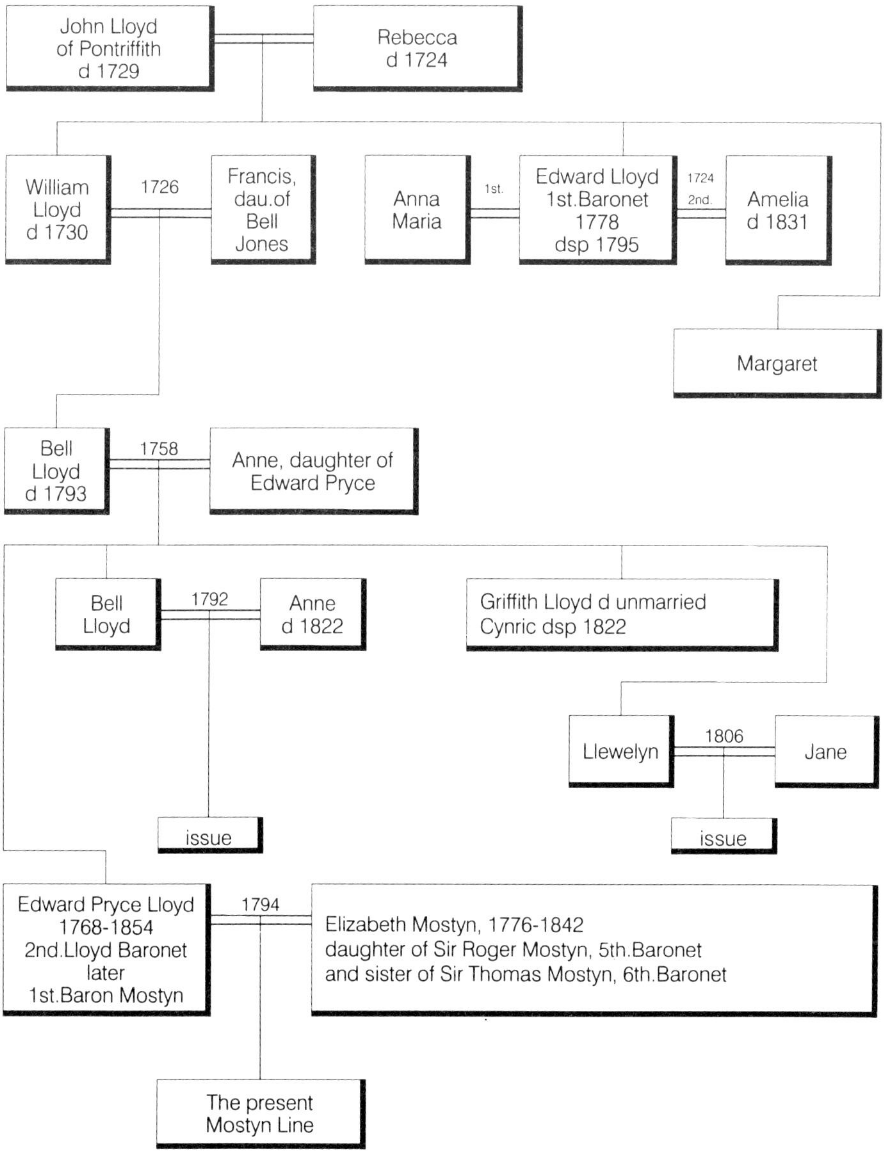

Key
b - born, **d** - died, **d unm** - died unmarried
dsp - decessit sine prole (died without issue)

The Mostyn Barons

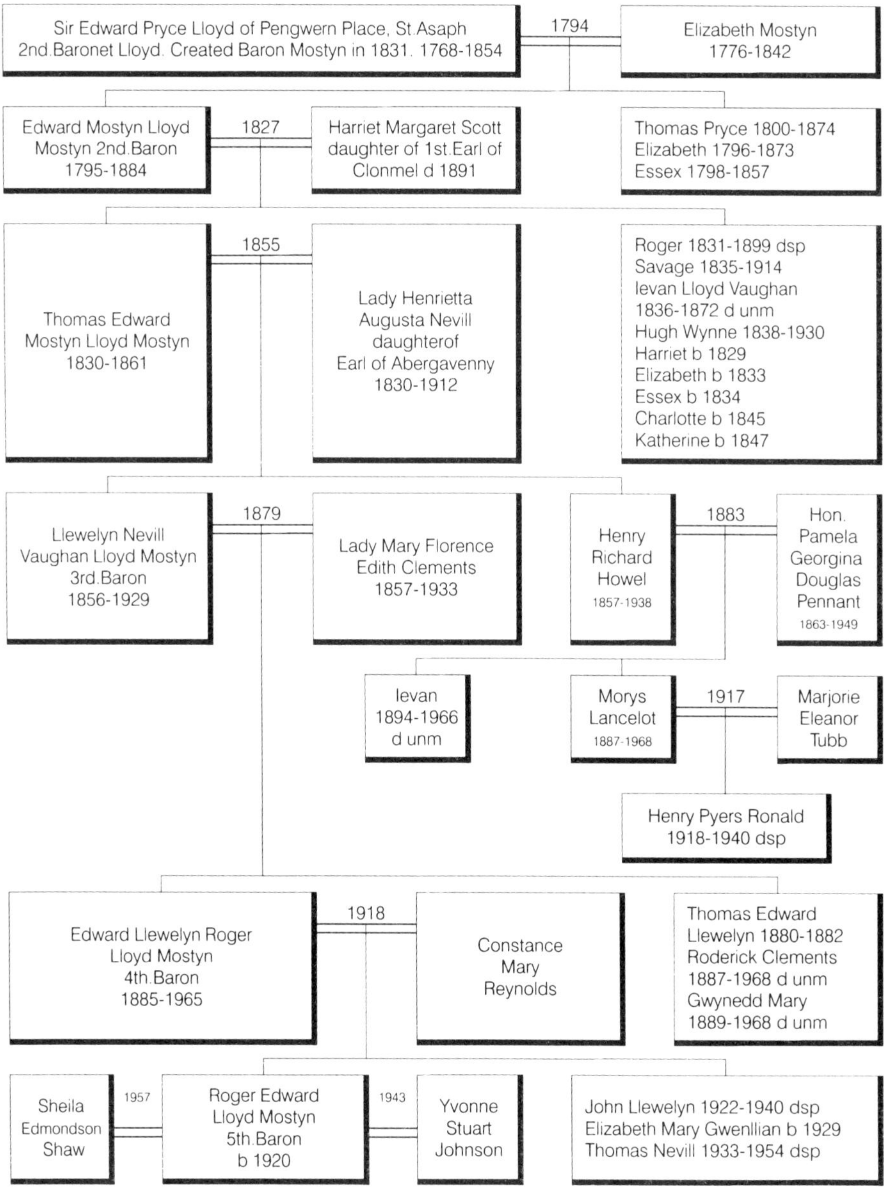

Key
b - born, **d** - died, **d unm** - died unmarried
dsp - decessit sine prole (died without issue)

Years for the Early Churches

Date	Anglican	Baptist	Calvinist	Wesleyan	Congreg-ational	Catholic
	St.Tudno					
1814			Ebeneser			
1815		Tabernacl				
1835		New Tabernacl				
1837			Ebeneser rebuilt	Caersalem		
1840	St.George					
1857					Christ	
1860		Horeb				
1861			Seilo	Lloyd St.		
1862		Zion				
1865	Holy Trinity					
1866				St.John		
1867						Ty Aildro (house)
1871				Ebeneser		

N.B. The name Ebeneser was used for the Calvinistic Church of 1815 in Bodhyfryd Road and later for the Wesleyan Church of 1871 in Lloyd Street.
An explanation of the circumstances under which the name Ebeneser was replaced by Seilo (Siloh) by the Calvinists is to be found in Methodistiaid Dosbarth Llandudno, by Benjamin Williams and J.Tudno Williams, Calvinistic Methodist Printing Office Carnarfon.1926.
Information of this source and a translation from the Welsh was provided by Tom Parry.

List of Illustrations

Figure	Description	Page
	Llandudno from the Great Orme	ii
	Llandudno from the Little Orme	iv
	Church Walks	viii
1	Llanrhos Church	7
2	Mostyn name announcement	11
3	Gloddaeth map - 1832	12
4	Creuddyn sketch map	19
5/6/7	Mostyn rent roll entries	20/21/22
8	Village sketch map	24
9	Enclosure Act	27
10	Ordnance map - 1840's	30
11	Brochure - 1849	34
12/13/14	Proposed Terrace, Villa and Hotel	35
15	Building Regulations	36
16	St.George's Harbour Act	39
17	Railway print	40
18	Improvement Act	42
19	Water Analysis	52
20/21	Rev.Evans purchase documents	56/57
22	Terms of lease	58
23	Building Regulations	59
24	Visitors' map - 1850's	61
25	Ordnance map - 1860's	62
26	Extracts from Bye-laws	63
27	Pritchard's Shop	65
28/29	St.George's Hotel purchase document	68/69
30	Gloddaeth Crescent	70
31	St.George's Hotel	70
32	Queen's Hotel	70
33	Cliff Walk	72
34	St.Tudno's Church	73
35	St.George's Church	75
36	Congregational Church	76
37	The Baths, as planned	81
38	The Baths and old Pier - photograph	81
39	Telegraph Station	82
40	Gloddaeth	86
41	Bodysgallen	87
42	Lifeboat launch	90
43	Improvement boundary	91
44	Pritchard advert	92
45	T.Williams advert	92
46	French Gloves advert	93
47	Cornaby advert	93
48	John Davies advert	93
	Llandudno Bay	104

Subject Index

A
Actons ... 93
Adwy Rydd ... 24
Atgofion Hen Llandudno ... 20,22,29

B
Baptists, early ... 73
Bardic references ... 2,3,85
Barnes, James ... 48
Bartley's Library ... 83
Bathing, nude ... 67
Baths ... 41,66,71,80,81,83
Birling Manor ... 89
Bishop of Bangor ... 2,13,28,52
Boatmen ... 65,72
Bodafon ... 11,24
Bodysgallen ... 2,8,85,87
Brass Band ... 72
Bridge's Circulating Library ... 84
British and Foreign School ... 78
Brookes, Wiliam ... 67
Brynyfelin ... 29
Brynia ... 25,91
Bryn y Bia ... 24
Building materials ... 68
Building Regulations ... 33,35,56,59
Burial grounds ... 77
Bye-laws ... 63,67,83

C
Caersalem ... 21,74,75
Catholic Chapel ... 77,80
Champneys,
  Sir Thomas Swymmer ... 10,11,13,14,86
  Dame Charlotte Mostyn 10,11,13,14,79,86
Child workers ... 23,30
Christ Church ... 76
Coast erosion ... 1,3,20
Colbran, J.H. ... 48
Compton House ... 84
Congregationalists ... 76
Cornaby's Photographic ... 92,93
Creuddyn ... 2,17,18,19
Croes Onen ... 21,23,78
Cryd Tudno ... 18
Cust, R.J. ... 71,89
Cwm Howard ... 18,91
Cwlach Street ... 22

D
Davies, Evan ... 64
Davies, Isaiah ... 68,69,70
Davies, John ... 64
Davies, John (Tailor) ... 92,93
Disinfectant powder ... 67

E
Ebeneser ... 74,76
Ellerby, Herbert ... 72,84
Ellis, Thomas P.W. ... 66
Enclosure
  Designated roads ... 29
  Description of the land ... 29
  General discussion ... 26,37
  Land allocation ... 28
  The 1843 Act ... 27
Evans, Rev.E.T. ... 48,55,56,57,77

F
Felton, George ... 71

G
Gas and Water Office ... 92
Gas lamps ... 54
Gas supply ... 54
George and Dragon ... 21
Gloddaeth
  Celebrationsof 1851 ... 87
  Doves at ... 3
  Meaning of ... 85
  Property Schedule of 1843
  ... 17,19,20,21,22,24,74
  Spelling of ... 85
  Tenants rent dinners ... 85
  Tree felling at ... 11,12
Gloddaeth Crescent ... 70
Gloddaeth Isa ... 25
Gogarth
  Farm ... 18,20
  Lease of land ... 13,16
  Spring ... 20,47,51,52,53
Greenhill ... 21
Gruffydd ap Rhys ... 1
Gwyther and Warden ... 70

H
Hafod y nos ... 23,38
Hen Gapel Bach ... 78
Herapeth, William ... 51,52
Holand ... 24
Homeopathic Depot ... 92
Horeb ... 75
Hughes, John ... 52
Hughes, William ... 66
Hydrants ... 53
Hydropathic Establishment ... 80

I
Improvement Commissioners
  Boundary ... 91
  Burials ... 77
  Bye-laws ... 63
  Devolvement of power ... 52,54
  Finances and loans ... 44-46
  First meeting ... 37,43
  Offices ... 92
  Pier location ... 41
  Powers ... 66

Sea defence 70,71
Sewerage and drainage plans . 47-49,60,61
Tribute to T.E.M.Ll.Mostyn 89
Inheritance, male line 8
Italian Warehouse 92

J
Johnson, Dr.Samuel 18
Jones, Thomas 86
Jones, William 28,32,74

K
King's Head 52,68
Knight, Edwin 48

L
Land auction 33
Land leases 55
Law Fire Office Co. 44,45,46
Liverpool Mercury 30
Llandudno
As a harbour port 31,39,41
As watering place 29,41,75
Attractions 34,92
Directory 84,92
Early accomodation 31,33
First large houses 55
First plans 33,35
Land prices 37,55
Leasehold tenure 35,37
Lifeboat 89,90
Population 18,66,91
Revised plans 47
Visitor 92
Llanrhos 2,5,6,7,79
Lloyd, Sir Edward Pryce
(1st.Baron Mostyn) 6,8,10,27
Lloyd, Gruffydd 6,8,16
Lloyd succession to title 8,10
London Gazette 10,71

M
Madoc Street housing 38
Maesdu 18,25,91
Maes y facrell 21
Maes y Maenllwyd 25
Margaret of Gloddaeth 1
Marine Parade 68
Market Hall 66,67,82
Medical attention at Gloddaeth 5
Methodists 73
Mines of Great Orme 18
Morfa Isa 18,23,29
Morfa Rhianedd 1,30,62
Morgan, Rev.John 77
Mostyn, Lady Augusta (see also Nevill) 88,89
Mostyns of XV,XVI Centuries 1,2,3
Mostyns of XVII, XVIII Centuries 3,4,5,6
Mostyn dispute over legacies 13
Mostyn, Hon.E.M.Lloyd
(later Second Baron Mostyn)
Accession to Barony 41,87
Agreement with Champneys 14
Conditions of land sale 58
Control of estates 15
Enclosure Act 27
Improvement Act 41
Land allocated 28
Land auction 33
Land exchange 74
Land holdings 28
Land usage 31
Marriage 62
Meeting with O.Williams 32
Reply to condolences 89
Residence at Gloddaeth 86
School site 79
St.George's Director 39,40
Trinity Church proposal 77,89
Mostyn, First Baron 10,11
Mostyn, Fifth Baronet 8,10,11,55
Mostyn, Miss Frances 79,86
Mostyn Mortgages 10,17,55
Mostyn Surname 2
Mostyn, Sir Thomas
(Sixth Baronet) 6,7,8,10,11,15,16,86
Mostyn, Hon.Thomas E.M.Lloyd
Commissioner 37,43,46,47,55
Early death 88,89
Land leases 55
Majority celebration 86
Marriage 43,62
M.P. 41
Street adoptions 60
Trinity Church proposal 77,89

N
National School 78
Nevill, Lady Henrietta Augusta
(Lady Augusta Mostyn) 43,62
Nicol, Dr.James 67
Nuisances 65,66

O
Officer of Health 67
Old Mine 52,53
Ormeshead 3,18

P
Parade, first houses 68
Parish Boundary 24,91
Parish road to Conway 29,60
Parry, R. 37
Parry, Thomas 66,83
Pen Morfa adit 23
Pentre Isa 24
Pen y Dinas 18

Pen y Mynydd . . . 21
Pier . . . 41, 71,81
Pinfold . . . 63
Plague . . . 1
Police
  Clothing . . . 65,67
  County Force . . . 66
  Early history . . . 63,64
  Inspector of Nuisances . . . 64,67
  Lockup . . . 65
  Parish Constable Act . . . 64
Polin, Edward . . . 64,65
Pony stand . . . 53,83
Powell, William . . . 84
Pritchard, Rev.Dr. . . . 30
Pritchard's shop . . . 65,91,92
Pwll y Gwichiad . . . 20,28

Q
Queen's Hotel . . . 68,70

R
Rabbit warrens . . . 23
Railway Station . . . 41,61,84
Rateable value . . . 45
Rate Collector . . . 45
Rates . . . 44
Reece, William Henry . . . 77
Rees, George . . . 66
Richard of Bodysgallen . . . 2
Roads
  Adoption . . . 56
  Grid System . . . 61
  Early state . . . 3,4
Roberts, John . . . 65
Rofft Bach . . . 63
Rowlands, Thomas . . . 19,29,38,74,77,78
Royalist support . . . 4

S
Schoolroom (first) . . . 23
Schools (early) . . . 78
School teachers . . . 23,78,79
Sea bathing . . . 33,47,63
Sea defences . . . 70,71
Seilo . . . 76
Smith, F.Macdougall . . . 47,48,49,52,53
Smith, John . . . 30
St.John's Church . . . 76,77
St.George's Church . . . 19,74,75,77
St.George's Hall . . . 77,84
St.George's Harbour Act . . . 39
St.George's Harbour & Railway Co.
  Aims . . . 31,39
  Damaged pier . . . 71
  Railway plans . . . 40,41,47
  Time limits . . . 41
St.George's Hotel . . . 29,68,70
St.George's School . . . 23,78
St.Tudno's Church . . . 18,74,77
Spinther, Dr.James . . . 74
Storms of 1839 . . . 18,74
Storms of 1859 . . . 71
Street adoption . . . 60
Street names . . . 56,60,61,62

T
Tabernacl . . . 21,74,75
Tai Newyddion . . . 22
Tambling (Tamblyn), Joseph . . . 22
Tan y Nant . . . 22
Telegraph Station . . . 81,82
Temperance Society . . . 74
Thomas,Owen . . . 68
Tom and Jerry device . . . 20,52
Turbary . . . 27
Turkish Baths . . . 80
Ty Draw . . . 20
Ty Glas . . . 22
Ty Gwyn . . . 21
Ty'n pwll . . . 23
Tyn y ffrith . . . 25,71,91
Tyn y hwlfa . . . 52
Ty Ucha . . . 24

W
Walcott, George . . . 54
Walters, John . . . 66
Water analysis . . . 51,52
Water and Gas Company . . . 53
Water shortage . . . 52,53
Water supply . . . 49-54
Wehnert and Ashdown . . . 47,70,80
Westmacott, Mr. 44-49,52,56,65,70,71,80,83
Williams, David . . . 45
Williams, Ellis . . . 56,57
Williams, John . . . 11,24,31,33,38,43,45
  and . . . 48,54,55,60,66,80,93
Williams, Owen . . . 29,31,33,35,37,68,80
Williams, Robert . . . 73,75
Williams, Thomas . . . 84,92
Worthington (mine lessees) . . . 22,74
Wyddfryd . . . 21
Wynn marriages . . . 2,3,6

Y
Yates, Richard . . . 28
Yr hen dafarn . . . 21
Y Rofft . . . 21

Z
Zion . . . 75,77

Llandudno Bay